Don't Get Married! Unless You Understand A Few Things First!

Anthony Ferraioli, M.D.

D0066934

CONTENTS

Dedicated to all couples who are trying to turn
their relationships into emotional laboratories...

INTRODUCTION

WHAT'S A MARRIAGE FOR ANYWAY?

O ver 10,000 hours of both individual and couples therapy work in my private practice have taught me that this is an important question to ask, and yet it is also a question which rarely *does* get asked before we marry.

Mind you, this question is different from asking ourselves whether or not we should marry *a particular person.* It is more fundamental than that. *This* question asks: Why am I getting married in the first place? What are my expectations from my spouse and from marriage in general?

What's a marriage for anyway?

Is marriage meant to express our true love? Is it for committing to a permanent, monogamous relationship with a "soulmate"? Is it to lay the foundation for having children and starting a family? Is it simply a cultural tradition passed down from generation to generation which we are expected to continue? Or is it for the excitement of the wedding ceremony itself?

I think that the reasons we marry may include a little bit of each of these, but I also know that it can be much more than that: *Marriage can and should be an opportunity for two people to work together to help each other grow to become the best individuals they can be.* Notice the use of the word *work*.

MARRIAGE CAN AND SHOULD BE AN OPPORTUNI-TY FOR TWO PEOPLE TO *WORK* TOGETHER TO HELP EACH OTHER GROW TO BE-COME THE BEST INDIVIDU-ALS THEY CAN BE.

Ask around and I'm pretty sure you'll find that most people won't say that they got married in order to *work*. Instead, words like "true love" and "soulmate" are often used, as in "he was my soulmate and true love but then we fell out of love...I still love him but I'm not *in love* with him."

Words like "true love" and "soulmate" can be very romantic and wonderful, but not necessarily very accurate or predictive of what actually happens in many marriages over time, even the ones which don't end in divorce. The widespread use of these words is the end result of our misunderstandings about the realities of why we marry versus what we *should* be looking for and doing with each other in a marriage.

> WORDS LIKE "TRUE LOVE" AND "SOULMATE" CAN BE VERY ROMANTIC AND WONDERFUL, BUT NOT NECESSARILY VERY ACCURATE OR PREDICTIVE OF WHAT ACTUALLY HAPPENS IN MANY MARRIAGES OVER TIME, EVEN THE ONES WHICH DON'T END IN DIVORCE.

Which is the reason why, in this book, you'll learn a very different language describing what marriage really can and should be. I will explain away the concepts of "true love" and "soulmate" which so often fade and betray us over time, leaving in their wake great amounts of disappointment, resentment, contempt and even repulsion between spouses.

I want to help you begin to see marriage in terms of new concepts like *Emotional Credibility* and *Emotional Connectedness;* ones which will guide us to unlocking the true joys and true purpose of marriage. You will learn about how your marriage is like an *Emotional Laboratory* where both you and your spouse are constantly driven to treat each other with the habits and behaviors you've each learned as children, and about how to use this laboratory to help each other grow and behave more like healthy, true adults with one another. And in this Emotional Laboratory of marriage, you will learn how to earn each others' Emotional Credibility, from which true marital bliss is born.

You will see that marriage is your chance to either heal from or continue to suffer from the hurts of your past. You will see that, in order to do it right, marriage takes *courage* and it requires *taking risks* with your spouse such as *learning to say and do things that are not your first reaction to say or to do;* things which may make you feel uncomfortable at first. And you will see that by doing these things, both you and your spouse will grow stronger than ever and so will your marriage.

IN ORDER TO DO IT RIGHT,
MARRIAGE TAKES *COURAGE*
AND IT REQUIRES *TAKING*
RISKS WITH YOUR SPOUSE
SUCH AS *LEARNING TO SAY*
AND DO THINGS THAT ARE
NOT YOUR FIRST REACTION
TO SAY OR TO DO.

You will come away thinking of your marriage as an *investment*, an Emotional Investment which becomes more and more valuable and irreplaceable the more you put into it using the specific ideas and concepts in this book.

And finally, I hope that the irony of the book's title and what may initially appear to be a cold, unromantic approach is not lost on you as you discover the true message that I am trying to convey to you: that marriage can be one of the most loving, most healing ways in which we can be there for another human being as well as for ourselves.

MARRIAGE CAN BE ONE OF
THE MOST LOVING, MOST

HEALING WAYS IN WHICH
WE CAN BE THERE FOR
ANOTHER HUMAN BEING AS
WELL AS FOR OURSELVES.

For, in the end, it is not that I don't believe in "soul mates" or "true love", and it's certainly not that I don't want you to get married. In fact, it's really just the opposite. However, I want to teach you how to do it the *right way* and I want to give you fair warning about how hard it is to do so.

In fact, in order to succeed at this, you will have to first abandon any thoughts of being able to stay the same person you are right now. Marriage, done the right way, demands that you *change as an individual. It demands that you grow and that you grow up.*

YOU WILL HAVE TO ABAN-
DON ANY THOUGHTS OF
BEING ABLE TO STAY THE
SAME PERSON YOU ARE
RIGHT NOW.

In my experience, the real hurdle to a happy marriage is that not many people are willing to do this, and even fewer understand that this is the central task of being a married person, i.e. to grow as an individual. I want you to be able to do both: to understand that to be married the right way, you must change as a person AND *to do it!*

After reading this book I hope you'll never need to say the words, "We just fell *out of love*", or "We love each other, but we're just not *in love*", ever again.

–A. Ferraioli, M.D.

CHAPTER 1

THE PROBLEM WITH MARRIAGE

First, and most importantly: if you are already married or are in a serious relationship, or, if you are even just *considering* starting a relationship with someone, please read the following very carefully:

> MARRIAGE IS NOT FOR CHILDLIKE ADULTS. IN-STEAD, IT IS FOR TRUE, EMOTIONALLY COMPETENT ADULT INDIVIDUALS.

Now if, after reading this, you've gathered that one must strive to become an emotionally competent *individual* in order to have a healthy marriage, then you are absolutely correct!

The simple truth is that you cannot have a healthy marriage without becoming a healthier adult yourself. And the sad fact is that most of us start out thinking that we are adults, when, in reality, we are simply *adult-looking*. We must know and understand this reality:

> BASED UPON OUR REAC-
> TIONS AND THE WAY WE
> BEHAVE, MOST OF US IN-
> ITIALLY QUALIFY ONLY AS
> *ADULT-LOOKING*, BUT NOT
> AS *TRUE, EMOTIONALLY
> COMPETENT ADULTS.*

Take a look at this statement:

> OUR BEHAVIOR IS WHAT'S
> HAPPENING WHEN WE'RE
> NOT PAYING ATTENTION.

We often take our behaviors and reactions for granted, and seldom do we take the time or expend the energy to truly *observe ourselves*, much less get to know *why* we behave the way that we do. Instead, we just go along on automatic pilot, shooting from the hip, reacting whichever way we please, as adult-hood simply becomes a continuation of childhood. (How about all those times your spouse has said or done something to you which triggered a strong emotional reaction which you then acted upon immediately either through words or behaviors?)

On the whole, marriage is not done very well these days at all, as evidenced by the fact that, depending on how much weight you place on such statistics, at least half of all marriages end in divorce. My professional experience has taught me that most marriages fall into three general categories:

The first group stays together long enough to celebrate their 60th wedding anniversary, but only because one spouse took up much of the slack of the other spouse's emotionally immature behaviors all those years. He or she just "hung in there" loyally, through all the "ups and downs", regardless of the personal cost to themselves. You'll often see depression, anxiety, or chronic physical ailments in the spouse who made all of the accommodations.

The other possibility with this first group is that they essentially lived separate lives while they were seemingly "together". They never actually grew into a truly mature, emotionally competent adult couple.

The second group divorces.

The third group, unlike the first, does, in fact, grow closer and more emotionally intimate over the years as they customize and *use the marriage* to grow as true, emotionally competent individuals.

> ...THEY CUSTOMIZE AND *USE THE MARRIAGE* TO GROW AS TRUE, EMOTION-ALLY COMPETENT INDIVID-UALS.

In my experience, this last group represents the minority of marriages.

And here's why:

When people get married, a strange thing happens:

> SOONER OR LATER, THEY BEGIN TO CHANGE FROM

PEER / PEER TO PARENT /
CHILD.

Now here's the thing: *Peers* treat each other with *unconditional positive regard,* i.e. the benefit of the doubt.   This is a mature and realistic goal in a marriage and promotes individual, adult growth.

Children, on the other hand, want *unconditional love,* like what they were supposed to get from their parents, and they continue to want this from their spouses.   When they eventually realize, either consciously or subconsciously, that it is not available to them in the marriage, resentments grow.

You see, *unconditional positive regard* means that we still have responsibility for our behaviors and what we do with strong emotions such as anger and disappointment. It is a very *adult* concept.

Unconditional love, on the other hand, means that we have no real responsibility for our behaviors or strong emotions. It means that we get to show the parent our "poopie diaper" and we expect them to clean it up for us without our help. This, unfortunately, is what many of us think we should get out of our marriages, a parent to clean up our poopie diaper.

Whether we realize it or not, this is the expectation we have of our spouse. That is, we expect the *unconditional love* that only a child can get from a mother, father, or other adult caregiver. Clearly, you can see where this expectation, often subconsciously acted out with unhealthy behaviors, can cause big problems in a marriage.

> WHEN WE CHANGE FROM
> *PEERS* TO *PARENT/CHILD*,
> RESENTMENTS GROW.

Every time one spouse acts in such a way that they have given up personal responsibility for their behavior or reactions, they are demonstrating their wish and expectation that the other spouse is the all loving, all forgiving, and unconditional love-giving parent.

At that very moment, the marriage is compromised and has shifted from the peer/peer model to the parent/child one.

What happens next is that the couple experiences first emotional disconnect, then, as the disconnect builds, physical disconnect as well (i.e. lack of sexual intimacy.)

When people get married, another strange thing happens:

> THEY GO FROM INITIALLY
> IDEALIZING EACH OTHER TO
> EVENTUALLY DEVALUING
> EACH OTHER.

In other words, when we first meet, we "fall in love." Then, as we spend more time together and become more like family, we "fall out of love." Now we are no longer happy together: First idealization, then devaluation.

We really only get to know each other in terms of what we wish the other person was (idealized view), or, later, what a disappointment the person is to us (devalued view.)

We never actually get to know the real person we are with, complete with good and bad parts. We lose the shades of gray and instead see our spouses in black and white terms, namely through initial idealization followed by devaluation of them.

Who we thought was our "soulmate" turns out to be nothing more than a huge disappointment to us for various reasons. Maybe it becomes about money, or maybe we feel bored or unchallenged, or perhaps it's that we've simply "fallen out of love."

Whatever the reasons look like on the surface, what has really happened is that we've never actually gotten to know the real person that we've chosen to be with. We've simply gone from the idealized image that we projected onto them (i.e. our expectations of them), down to the devalued, "all bad" view of them (i.e. all the disappointments.)

This pattern can, and often does, repeat itself multiple times with successive significant others, all the while leaving us blind to the reality of what's really going on as we search for happiness by trying over and over again to choose the right "soulmate".

IN THE PROCESS, TRUE
ADULTHOOD IS LOST TO
THE WISH FOR SOME OTHER

"IDEAL" PERSON TO FIX OUR
LIVES AND MAKE US HAPPY.

The fact of the matter is that, although there are most certainly some truly bad seeds out there, and, also, that we do sometimes choose spouses in such a dysfunctional manner as to make the resulting relationship unfixable; it is also true that in many cases we just simply never choose to *stop* and *ask* ourselves what our role is in making the good or bad parts come forward in the other person; i.e., in *triggering the other person's buttons as they trigger ours.* Both spouses need to ask themselves this question if we are to heal as individuals and heal the marriage. More on this later.

Try this exercise: imagine that your significant other has just triggered a strong emotional reaction in you. This can be anger, fear, anxiety, envy, distrust, shame, guilt, whatever. Now, imagine your response. What did you imagine?

Did you react *automatically* on your strong emotion; i.e. angrily, fearfully, anxiously, guiltily, etc.?

Or, did you hold back a moment, use *restraint*, and try communicate to your spouse what you were feeling as best you can?

> DO YOU TRY TO USE *RE-STRAINT*, AS YOU ATTEMPT TO COMMUNICATE TO YOUR SPOUSE WHAT YOU FEEL AS BEST YOU CAN?

Most of the time, it is exquisitely difficult to do the latter, so that the great majority of us do the former; i.e. we *react* to one another in childlike, impulsive, and *unrestrained* ways.

We then lose what I call Emotional Credibility with each other (a word which is a combination of *trusting* and actually *liking* the other person and wanting to have them around you); resentments and distrust grow as the walls come up between us.

As the integrity of the relationship then begins to break down, both spouses are at even higher risk for acting out behaviors such as affairs, spending, risk-taking, workaholism, drugs and alcohol, angry outbursts, or passive-aggressive behaviors. The destructive cycle feeds itself and becomes self-sustaining: The more we disappoint each other with our reactivity, the more we lose Emotional Credibility with each other, and the more we act out our feelings of rejection, anger, abandonment, and betrayal.

> THE MORE WE DISAPPOINT EACH OTHER WITH OUR REACTIVITY, THE MORE WE LOSE EMOTIONAL CREDIBILITY WITH EACH OTHER, AND THE MORE WE ACT OUT OUR FEELINGS OF REJECTION, ANGER, ABANDONMENT, AND BETRAYAL.

You might want to think of a strong, whole marriage as a lifeboat without any leaks in it. As the storms of life hit each of us (money problems, health problems, child raising issues, work stresses, etc.), a marriage in which each individual has worked on *themselves* and has built Emotional Credibility with the other helps us both survive and even thrive.

On the other hand, a marriage which has lost its integrity is not only a leaky boat, but is also prone to capsizing. What I mean is that, as the resentments and disconnects grow, the risk of acting out behaviors is actually *higher* in the marriage than it would be if the couple were not together at all.

> A MARRIAGE WHICH HAS
> LOST ITS INTEGRITY IS NOT
> ONLY A LEAKY BOAT, BUT IS
> ALSO PRONE TO CAPSIZING.

In other words, as the marriage becomes more and more unhealthy the relationship becomes more and more toxic to each spouse and can actually function as a trigger for acting out behaviors in each of them. Now, instead of helping each spouse heal and grow, the marriage becomes a detriment and a danger to each of them.

Let's continue to focus on the individual's role in creating happiness or misery in their lives with the following statement:

WE HUMANS ACTIVELY RE-
CREATE THE EMOTIONAL
POSITIONS OF OUR CHILD-
HOODS (I.E. HELPLESSNESS,
REJECTION, VICTIMHOOD,
POWERLESSNESS, FEARFUL-
NESS, GUILT, FEELING
OVERWHELMED, CHAOS,
ETC.) WITH OUR SPOUSES
THE CLOSER WE GET TO
THEM AND THE MORE THEY
BECOME LIKE FAMILY TO US.

We do this by immediately acting out our emotional reactions to them when they trigger us. This is a childlike behavior and it recreates childhood misery and preserves our unhappiness. When we feel a strong emotion and instantly react to it, we add our fifty-percent to the misery about to be created between ourselves and our spouses. And we recreate our own childhood misery for ourselves by placing ourselves back into the emotional positions of our childhoods as I've listed in the above statement.

WHEN WE FEEL A STRONG
EMOTION AND INSTANTLY
REACT TO IT, WE ADD OUR
FIFTY-PERCENT TO THE MI-
SERY ABOUT TO BE
CREATED BETWEEN OUR-
SELVES AND OUR SPOUSES.

The problem is that we then blame the other person, or the circumstances, for our misery. If we are each doing this in our marriage then you can see how we are each contributing to the preservation of our misery. We are each wanting the other person to get fixed or to fix us, rather than acknowledging and addressing our fifty-percent of the problem, i.e. our own reactions and behaviors.

WE ARE EACH WANTING THE
OTHER PERSON TO GET
FIXED OR TO FIX US, RA-
THER THAN ACKNOWLEDG-
ING AND ADDRESSING OUR
FIFTY-PERCENT OF THE
PROBLEM, I.E. OUR OWN

REACTIONS AND BEHA-
VIORS.

I cannot emphasize this last point enough. When we marry, we are subconsciously asking the other person to fix us or fix our lives and make it whole again. We take on the role of the victim-child and set our expectations at an unrealistic and unfair level that is doomed to fail; all because we continue to live under the assumption that the other person or the circumstances need to change, in order for us to be happy or healed.

Instead, I want you to consider this:

MARRIAGE IS BUT AN EMO-
TIONAL LABORATORY FOR
TWO INDIVIDUALS WHO
HAVE CHOSEN TO BE TO-
GETHER.

This laboratory can be very effective in helping us gather data about ourselves by allowing us to observe how we react and behave towards our spouses. This way we can learn, among other things, more about our role in preserving and repeating our misery.

For example, if we're paying attention and trying to observe ourselves in the Emotional Laboratory of marriage, we will learn about the strong emotions we may have which trigger reactions and behaviors towards our spouses. Let's call these emotional reactions our "buttons."

These buttons were not created by our spouses, but, instead, from our childhood experiences with our parents and families of origin. *Spouses push each others' buttons but did not create them.*

> SPOUSES PUSH EACH OTH-
> ERS' BUTTONS BUT DID NOT
> CREATE THEM.

Please go ahead and read that last statement again: *Spouses push each others' buttons but did not create them.* The problem is that we *do* blame our spouses for creating those miserable buttons, whether we are aware of it consciously or not.

In fact, we blame them for pretty much everything that makes us unhappy to some extent or another. When Sally criticizes Johnny's choice of whatever, Johnny may not be hearing the criticism for what it is in the here and now; he may also be feeling, at a deeper, subconscious level, a sense of rejection or shame, which is a button for him that was created in childhood.

Now, Sally didn't create that button for Johnny, but Johnny's reaction will almost certainly not take that into account. No, he will, in fact, *take it personally and react to it*, and that's how we know a button has been pushed. And you know he will.

Ideally, what would happen once that button is pushed is that, instead of immediately reacting, Johnny would have some sense that he's been triggered, and that, though Sally pushed a button, she's not the one who put it there. He would realize that he's at high risk of overreacting because he's feeling some very strong emotions like he did when he was a kid with whomever initially put that button there in the first place.

This can be a reaction of fear, anger/rage, shame/humiliation, helplessness, powerlessness, you name it. And it'll come with a sense of urgency and high stakes which will make him want to or even "need to" act immediately (think fight or flight.)

Johnny might instead resist the urge to react and instead tell Sally that this is a button for him which he's working on.

Sally should then respond with empathy and understanding rather than defending herself or her actions. In her mind she should be thinking about the bigger picture of this being a button for her spouse which started in his childhood and which the marriage can now help heal, depending, in part, on her reaction right now. Johnny has helped her to be able to do this for him by changing *his* initial reaction to begin with and not attacking her.

Instead of reinforcing each others' initial, childlike reactions, Sally and Johnny are working hard together, as individuals, to change history by using each other and the Emotional Laboratory of marriage to heal from the past.

So much for the ideal outcome.

What really happens is that Johnny goes with his first reaction, then Sally gets defensive, then so does Johnny in return, and we're off to the races!

COUPLES EXPECT THAT THEIR SPOUSES WILL NOT PUSH THEIR BUTTONS BE- CAUSE THEY ARE "SOUL- MATES" OR BECAUSE THEY ARE "IN LOVE." THEN, WHEN THEY DO, THEY DEVALUE AND BLAME EACH OTHER, AND THE WALL BETWEEN THEM GROWS.

In the marriage laboratory, we have an opportunity to begin to heal our buttons by viewing our spouses as simply the latest triggers of these buttons, not the cause. By behaving more empathetically and adult-like, we are using marriage to heal ourselves and our spouses by changing our reactions and behaviors towards one another. The goal is to help each other to heal from the triggers of childhood instead of immediately reacting to them thereby relinquishing any possibility of change and growth.

The task, then, is to begin to recognize when we are being triggered and to communicate this to our spouse, who should then not argue or become defensive, but instead empathize with us. (It is often quite valuable for each spouse to do some therapy work around learning to identify when they are being triggered and how to describe those feelings to another person.)

Meanwhile, with all this work to be done in a marriage:

WE INSTEAD GO AROUND SEARCHING FOR AND WAITING FOR OUR "SOULMATES" OR "TRUE LOVES."

What we do not want to hear is that the concept of "soulmates" is not really what marriage is about. If I had a dollar for every time someone told me one of the following two things, I'd be that pro-verbial "rich man" right now:

"We just fell out of love. I mean we love each other, but we're just no longer in love with each other."

And:

"We're just not soulmates."

To these folks I offer the following harsh truth:

TRUE LOVE IS ABOUT AC-CEPTING OUR ROLES IN RE-CREATING OUR OWN MI-SERY AND IT IS ABOUT TRY-ING TO CHANGE THIS IN OURSELVES. ONLY THEN CAN WE TRULY EXPERIENCE BEING "IN LOVE" OR HAVING A "SOULMATE".

True love is about working hard to neutralize our strong reactions so that we do not add our fifty-percent to the perpetuation of the problem.

True love is about adult responsibility and working on our initial reactions. It is not about the childhood wish for unconditional love from the perfect parent, which will never happen. Your spouse can never be your perfect parent.

Another harsh reality:

> NEITHER SPOUSE IS A REF-
> ERENCE POINT FOR PERFECT
> EMOTIONAL HEALTH AND
> TRUE, ADULT EMOTIONAL
> COMPETENCE.

When we react to the other person with immediate anger or disappointment, we are often subconsciously holding them to this standard rather than seeing them in some ways as imperfect childlike adults just as we ourselves are. In reality, they are really just somebody else's messed up kid!

Instead, we are wanting them to be the perfect, emotionally competent adult or *parent* to us, which they can never be.

WE LOSE OUR ROLE AS
THEIR PEER, AND BECOME
INSTEAD THE DISAP–
POINTED AND ANGRY CHILD
AS THEY BECOME THE IN–
COMPETENT PARENT IN
OUR EYES.

This role change leads to more resentment, and a bigger wall of disconnect between spouses. And when we lose the peer role and assume the child role, we also resume and reinforce all of our child-hood powerlessness and victimhood.

Another common problem with marriage is that people get married thinking that they will never be alone or feel lonely again.

To them I offer the following:

MARRIAGE IS NOT A CURE
FOR LONELINESS.

And yet, that is exactly why so many people get married, whether they realize it consciously or not. They think that, by getting married, they now have a guaranteed partner for all of their ups and downs in life.

Is this assumption true?

Well, sort of yes, but mostly no.

The problem with this assumption is that it is unrealistic and it creates an unfair demand on the spouse which can lead to resentments and disconnect.

And if the couple stays together, it is because the other person is so used to this demand from their own childhood experience that they do not understand that it's a problem. In other words, they are so used to their parents or other caregivers also putting them in the unfair position of being responsible for other people's loneliness, worry, pain, etc., that they continue to accept this responsibility in their marriage as well.

In this scenario, what eventually happens is that the couple ceases to be a relationship of peers and begins instead to take on the flavor of a child/parent relationship.

> WE MUST REALIZE THAT
> MARRIAGE IS NOT A GUAR-
> ANTEE FOR SEAMLESS COM-
> PANIONSHIP FOR THE REST
> OF OUR LIVES.

Each person is an individual, with their own buttons and needs for the healing of those buttons. This includes how much or how little closeness they need or choose to have at any given time. Getting to know each other in this way and respecting each other's needs promotes true, adult emotional intimacy in a marriage. Otherwise, one spouse might feel suffocated and drained by the unchecked dependency of the other.

Yet another fundamental problem with how we do marriage is not realizing the following:

> MARRIAGE IS AN ACTIVE,
> NOT A STATIC PROCESS.

You cannot marry a person and expect that they will remain the same for the next however many years. As each person begins to heal their buttons, they will evolve, as will the marital relationship.

It is never possible for only one person to evolve and not the other if a marriage is to grow stronger. A mature marriage consists of two individuals in search of healing from their individual childhood buttons.

> A MATURE MARRIAGE CONSISTS OF TWO INDIVIDUALS IN SEARCH OF HEALING FROM THEIR INDIVIDUAL CHILDHOOD BUTTONS.

And as I've said earlier, a mature marriage is an Emotional Laboratory for the healing of two individuals from each of their past experiences. A mature marriage is an exquisitely customized and dynamic relationship wherein anything can be said and worked through because of the *high degree of what I call Emotional Credibility (which we'll get to more later) between the spouses.*

A mature marriage is one in which we stop doing to the other person what their caregivers did to them in childhood, so that they can finally heal from their buttons and patterns of defensive or destructive behaviors, in part because of our help.

I want to elaborate this with three ideas:

Number one:

> IF WE ARE TO HEAL WITHIN THE EMOTIONAL LABORATORY OF MARRIAGE, WE NEED TO TAKE CHANCES WITH OUR SPOUSES BY SAYING AND DOING THINGS THAT WE WOULD NORMALLY NOT SAY OR DO. EVEN SIMPLE THINGS LIKE "THANK YOU" AND "I'M SORRY".

Number two:

> NEXT, IF SOMETHING IS DIFFICULT TO SAY, WE

> MUST WORK ON HEALING
> OURSELVES ENOUGH TO BE
> ABLE TO SAY IT, WHICH
> WILL HELP US HEAL EVEN
> MORE.

And number three:

> IF SOMETHING IS DIFFICULT
> TO DO, WE MUST WORK ON
> HEALING OURSELVES
> ENOUGH TO BE ABLE TO DO
> IT, WHICH WILL HELP US
> HEAL EVEN MORE.

How hard is it for you to say "Thank you" to your spouse?

How about "I'm sorry"?

How hard is it for you to truly *listen* to them when they are talking to you, rather than jumping ahead to your own *comments* or agendas? (As in practicing my LVAC mnemonic from my book *LVAC Nation!* where LVAC™ stands for Listen, Validate, Ask, *then* Comment.)

How hard is it for you to not immediately blame or become angry or disappointed with your spouse or to not have an angry, blaming, or dismissive *tone?*

> TAKE CHANCES BY CHANG-
> ING YOUR BEHAVIORS TO-
> WARDS YOUR SPOUSE AND
> YOU WILL HEAL AS AN INDI-
> VIDUAL.

Our exploration of the problems with marriage thus far has gotten us to the following question:

How can we maximize each other's joy in a marriage?

> THE ANSWER IS THAT WE
> CAN MAXIMIZE EACH OTH-
> ER'S JOY IN A MARRIAGE BY
> ASSUMING RESPONSIBILITY
> FOR OURSELVES AND FOR
> OUR EMOTIONAL HEALING,

NOT BY IMPOSING CHILD-
LIKE EXPECTATIONS ON
OUR SPOUSES.

It is also important to promote happiness and joy for each other in a marriage. Support each other's individual growth and healing and you will be supporting your own growth and healing as well.

With this in mind:

DO NOT ATTEMPT TO CON-
TROL EACH OTHER. PRO-
MOTE THE OPPOSITE OF
THIS; FREEDOM OF EXPRES-
SION OF THE OTHER PER-
SON'S **TRUE SELF**, WHO
THEY REALLY ARE INSIDE.

And also:

DO NOT ATTEMPT TO
BLAME EACH OTHER. PRO-
MOTE THE OPPOSITE OF
THIS; FORGIVENESS AND

YOUR OWN PERSONAL RE-
SPONSIBILITY.

And finally:

DO NOT ATTEMPT TO IM-
POSE YOUR AGENDAS ON
ONE ANOTHER. PROMOTE
THE OPPOSITE OF THIS AS
WELL AS THE COMMUNICA-
TION REQUIRED IN THIS
PURSUIT, AND BECOME
EACH OTHER'S ABSOLUTE
BEST, MOST VALUABLE ALLY
AND SUPPORTER IN LIFE.

Now I will list out a few summarizing statements from this chapter before we move on. Please read and reread these statements until they become very familiar as it will help you get the most out of the rest of the book:

Get married only if you understand that marriage is an Emotional Laboratory for each individual's emotional growth and healing from their childhood buttons.

Get married only if you understand that marriage is NOT a cure for loneliness.

Get married only if you understand that you will need to take risks and behave differently than you normally would if you are to grow within your marriage and grow your marriage.

Get married only if you are willing to abandon the childhood idea of Unconditional Love from your caregivers for the adult idea of Unconditional Positive Regard from your peer, in other words, the benefit of the doubt.

Get married only if you can accept that you contribute fifty-percent to the misery of your current reality.

Get married only if you are prepared to not treat your spouse as a reference point for perfect adult emotional health so that you'll become resentful when they are not.

Get married only if you know that, by getting married, you will be making the other person "family", which will eventually make you the victim-child *and they the incompetent parent in your eyes and vice versa. This will trigger resentment in each of you.*

Get married only if you accept that marriage is an active, dynamic relationship with the true goal of each individual's emotional healing and therefore the maturation and joy of the marital relationship.

And finally:

GET MARRIED ONLY IF YOU
ARE WILLING AND ABLE TO
FORGIVE: FORGIVENESS OF
YOURSELF AND FORGIVE–
NESS OF YOUR SPOUSE.

Anger can be an addictive emotion, since its seeds often go way back to true, childhood injustices. Because of this, we forget to forgive. We forget to let it go.

So, in other words, get married only if you feel capable of healing enough to not forget to forgive. Otherwise, please don't do it.

In the end, if you are thinking about getting married or are already married, good luck, for it is potentially the best, most wonderful and miraculous relationship and vehicle for true, adult emotional healing; that is, IF you understand these few things first.

Good job getting through this very long chapter. I know it wasn't easy. Now you're prepared for chapter 2 and the rest of the book!

CHAPTER 2

WHAT TO DO: AN OVERVIEW

Firstly, and before we begin our discussion of what to do, you should know that we pick our spouses specifically because we fit each other *perfectly wrongly.*

In other words, your emotional issues, i.e. where your buttons are from the previous chapter, yolk perfectly with those of your spouse, so it is virtually a guarantee that you will eventually drive each other crazy; and not in a good way.

> IN A MARRIAGE, IT IS VIR-
> TUALLY A GUARANTEE
> THAT WE WILL EVENTUALLY
> DRIVE EACH OTHER CRAZY,
> AND NOT IN A GOOD WAY.

You see, in choosing our spouses, we have subconsciously found the perfect partner with whom to continue our childhood, complete with them hurting us and us hurting them in ways we are both familiar with from the past, at least subconsciously. This is what normally happens in an otherwise "innocent" marriage where there is just a lack of knowledge of the things we're talking about in this book; where our behaviors and reactions remain unchecked and unprocessed.

If abandonment and humiliation are part of your childhood background, then, guess what? You'll select for this type of treatment subconsciously in the spouse you choose.

If being controlled and having no power or autonomy were part of the deal you got as a youngster, guess what again? Yep, you'll select for these features in your choice of spouse.

In other words, rest assured that, while none of us would ever choose our spouses *consciously* in a way to cause us harm, almost all of us choose our spouses *subconsciously* to put us back into the painful emotional positions of our childhoods. Sound crazy? I agree, but that's also why I find my work ever so endlessly fascinating.

Now, on the bright side, since we go through all that trouble "picking" the exact person with whom we feel subconsciously "comfortable" for all the wrong reasons, (i.e. because they help trigger in us the same painful emotions and reactions as our caregivers originally did), we now have the perfect partner with whom we can *reverse* these hurts and heal from them by behaving differently towards each other than the way we were treated in our respective childhoods.

Here, since this is so important, let's say it again together:

> SINCE WE GO THROUGH SO MUCH TROUBLE SUB-CONSCIOUSLY "PICKING" THE EXACT PERSON WITH WHOM WE CAN CONTINUE OUR CHILDHOODS, WE NOW ALSO HAVE THE PERFECT PARTNER WITH WHOM WE CAN *REVERSE* THESE HURTS AND HEAL FROM THEM.

Okay, so now that we've chosen the exact wrong/right person, how do we go about using your marriage as a healing Emotional Laboratory to reverse each other's hurts and heal as individuals? In other words, what do we do?

Let me get us on the right track by giving you two extremely important pieces of advice right away:

Important Piece of Advice Number One: better to keep some of the formality in your marriage than to simply act any way you want to at any given moment.

Important Piece of Advice Number Two: better to be a "couple of relative strangers" who actually like each other and want to be together and can talk with each other than to become too much like "family" who have no choice but to love each other because they are related.

You'll see later on in chapter 7 (Sex and Marriage) that it is better to err on the side of being polite, caring "strangers" who like each other and choose to be together than to become de facto replacements for each other's family of origin. If you are able to do the former, you'll keep that all elusive "spark" alive, including sexually, in your marriage, but if you become each other's "family" than you'll eventually start to feel towards each other the way you did towards your family of origin as a child. All of the formalities and adult respect will then be replaced by childlike boundarylessness, angry demands, and unfair or unreasonable expectations of one another and the eventual repulsion that comes with this change, both emotionally *and* physically. (Remember the change from the peer/peer model to the parent/child one from chapter 1?)

"Strangers" who like each other and can talk to one another and choose to be together can feel warmly and share emotional *and physical* intimacy with each other forever; "family" really cannot. How else could we explain how much nicer and more polite and considerate most of us are to complete strangers or to acquaintances than we are to our own spouses and families? And how else can we explain the allure to have an affair in order to rekindle one's sex life and feelings of being special to someone again?

"STRANGERS" WHO LIKE
EACH OTHER AND CHOOSE
TO BE TOGETHER CAN FEEL

WARMLY AND SHARE EMO-
TIONAL *AND PHYSICAL* IN-
TIMACY WITH EACH OTHER
FOREVER; "FAMILY" REALLY
CANNOT.

N ow, with all of this in mind, let's start off with a quick little trick I've used with many couples with extremely good results. Its aim is to quickly reintroduce some of that formality and politeness I was just talking about back into your marriage.

This is a nice, simple technique I like to call the "Say Something Positive To Your Spouse Technique" and it promotes the kind of goodwill, respect, and formality which helps eventually lead to greater intimacy with each other. It goes like this:

Each time you are with your spouse, force yourself to say one positive thing.

It can be about anything you want.

It can be about the meal, the weather, work, the kids, the lawn, whatever.

The important point is that you get into the habit of letting your spouse experience you as a positive force in their life, not a negative, miserable one from their childhood.

THE IMPORTANT POINT IS THAT YOU GET INTO THE HABIT OF LETTING YOUR SPOUSE EXPERIENCE YOU AS A POSITIVE FORCE IN THEIR LIFE, NOT A NEGATIVE, MISERABLE ONE FROM THEIR CHILDHOOD.

This technique will, over time, help rebuild the trust, or what I call the Emotional Credibility in the marriage, which is like an emotional "points system" that I'll discuss more in chapter 6.

When you have a good amount of Emotional Credibility, the relationship is a healthy, healing relationship for both of you. When you do not have Emotional Credibility there is no trust, and, therefore, little, if any, good will and generosity between you. The emotional disconnect will then continue, and both emotional and physical intimacy will disappear.

But by committing yourself to using this simple little technique, you will begin to build emotional "points" with your spouse and they will, in turn and deep inside of their hearts, begin to feel like they are with someone they *want to be around.* They will also, quite naturally, feel more emotionally connected, trusting, and generous with you in return.

If we think about it for a moment, in a deeper, subconscious sense, you will be different from their overwhelmed, anxious, constantly upset or worried parents which will make you very attractive to them.

> YOU WILL BE DIFFERENT FROM THEIR OVER–WHELMED, ANXIOUS, CON–STANTLY UPSET OR WOR–RIED PARENTS WHICH WILL MAKE YOU VERY ATTRAC–TIVE TO THEM.

What you won't be doing is helping to continue the pain and powerlessness of their childhood for them, or for yourself. The two of you, individually and as a couple, will begin to heal with this little trick.

Next, I want to give you another piece of advice:

You must actually behave yourself with your spouse.

As I touched upon previously, and contrary to popular practice, in a marriage you really can't just "let it fly" and say or do anything you want at any given time. And as I mentioned in chapter 1, our behavior is what's happening when we're not paying attention.

> IN A MARRIAGE YOU REALLY
> CAN'T JUST "LET IT FLY"
> AND SAY OR DO ANYTHING
> YOU WANT AT ANY GIVEN
> TIME.

Here are a few things to consider:

First, you can't just fool around with your spouse any time you want to like you would with a friend or sibling, because a marriage is different from these other relationships. For one thing, there is that constant, dynamic up and down of Emotional Credibility which I briefly mentioned before and which you'll see again in chapter 6. It's sort of analogous to the stock market or a bank account; your balance (of Emotional Credibility points) goes up or down depending on how you behave each day. How your spouse feels about you, both in terms of emotional *and physical* intimacy, is directly related to your Emotional Credibility (trust + likability) with them.

Next, you must actually *follow through* on things in a responsible, thoughtful manner. Yes, you can disappoint your spouse and not have it be the end of the world, but, in general, what you say you'll do and what you've agreed to do had better be what you actually do. Blowing off your spouse is a very bad thing to do and will lose lots of Emotional Credibility points for you.

> WHAT YOU SAY YOU'LL DO
> AND WHAT YOU'VE AGREED
> TO DO HAD BETTER BE
> WHAT YOU ACTUALLY DO.

Furthermore, you must actually *think about your spouse* even when you're not with them and even when you don't immediately need something from them.

So, if you see a full garbage bag ready to be taken out, don't wait for your spouse to do it. Think about the Emotional Credibility points you're building by doing things like this for them; things that show that you are thinking about them and that you truly care about them enough to want to help them out.

If there's something (or several things) that you know your spouse would like or that would make their lives a little easier, do it for them. Again, you're investing in the relationship by building trust, or Emotional Credibility with them.

> IF THERE'S SOMETHING (OR
> SEVERAL THINGS) THAT
> YOU KNOW YOUR SPOUSE
> WOULD LIKE OR THAT
> WOULD MAKE THEIR LIVES A
> LITTLE EASIER, DO IT FOR
> THEM.

And *please* don't wait for a "thank you" every time to confirm that you should keep doing those things; just do them anyway. Yes, saying "thank you" as well as "I'm sorry" are both somewhat rare events in most marriages and need to be said more, but, for heaven's sake, don't allow yourself to react in a retaliatory manner to the absence of these words.

Keep doing the right thing by your spouse as long as they are trying to do the same for you. (In fact, if you haven't realized it by now, they should also read this book so that you can *both* be working on yourselves, and, therefore, on the marriage together as well.)

As a final aside and reminder before we move on, I want to reiterate that you shouldn't only do things for your spouse or treat them kindly and with respect when you immediately want or need something in return from them. The classic case is the husband who behaves like a true, emotionally competent adult man for one evening because he wants sex from his spouse, like, that night. This will actually lose for you a great amount of Emotional Credibility points, so please don't do it!

Another vital thing to know is this:

You have to watch your tone with your spouse.

A fast way to lose Emotional Credibility and to trigger your spouse's defenses is with an angry, sarcastic, blaming, shaming, or dismissive tone.

Your tone will set the tone between you.

Practice getting familiar with your tone. The easiest way to do this is to start to tune in more to your emotions when you speak with people, for your emotional state dictates your tone and people can instantly read it.

PRACTICE GETTING FAMILI-
AR WITH YOUR TONE.

The simple truth is that, other than facial expression and body language, our tone is the first sign we give to the world of our inner emotional state. For example, if you're angry, you won't really be able to hide it. Even if you make your voice sound sickeningly sweet in an attempt to hide your anger, it will creep the other person out and they'll sense it. And even if they don't fully know why on a conscious level, they will not feel at ease with you on a deeper, instinctive level and they will know something's up.

So as you become more and more aware of your emotional state when you are speaking with someone (am I angry?, anxious?, worried?, jealous?, fearful?, etc.), you will be more able to know how your tone will reflect and communicate those feelings to the other person. You'll know that, whether consciously or subconsciously, they've registered your tone and it will affect the Emotional Credibility and comfort level between you.

As you see, working on your tone means working on your general understanding of your emotional state at any given time. Especially when speaking with your spouse, a growing awareness of tone is extremely important for both of you.

WORKING ON YOUR TONE
MEANS WORKING ON YOUR
GENERAL UNDERSTANDING
OF YOUR EMOTIONAL
STATE AT ANY GIVEN TIME.

t is also vital that I tell you that (and I'm sure you're just going to *love* this one):

If you want a happy life, bring it yourself.

Okay, if you're still with me and you haven't thrown this book into your fireplace yet then know also that:

There is no such thing as the perfect husband or wife; there is only a partner whom you have chosen because you perfectly fit each other's emotional hurts from the past.

You must now settle in to the fact that it is time to work on *yourself*– your tone, your ability to *restrain* your impulses to react immediately, your LVAC™ (which stands for Listen, Validate, Ask, Comment– more on this later), and all the other "adult skills" necessary to carry on a relationship in a healthy, truly Emotionally Competent manner, no matter who it is with.

YOU MUST SETTLE IN TO
THE FACT THAT IT IS TIME
TO WORK ON *YOURSELF*.

You must not convince yourself that it's all your spouse's fault until you work on your fifty percent of the dynamic. (Remember from chapter 1 that we contribute fifty percent to the perpetuation of our own misery?)

Here are some examples of the issues which require working on yourself:

First, if you act in ways that frighten or intimidate your spouse or your children, you must stop doing this. When we induce fear in others, we give them a choice to make: they can either become a victim or they can become aggressive. Ultimately this breeds contempt and much loss of Emotional Credibility. If you have a problem with anger, you must work on *restraint* and other key adult skills. Just because you *can* yell or act out physically, does not mean that you should. *So restrain yourself.*

RESTRAIN YOURSELF.

Next, if you have a problem with addiction, seek professional help for it. *You cannot have a successful marriage with an active addiction issue.* It makes little difference what your addiction is, though some are more immediately destructive than others;

whether it's gambling, sex, alcohol or drugs, adventure and extreme risk taking, workaholism, or whatever else, it needs to be dealt with in a focused, deliberate manner. This can mean anything from an inpatient rehabilitation program, to participating in one of the multitude of excellent, free, twelve-step programs out there.

YOU CANNOT HAVE A SUCCESSFUL MARRIAGE WITH AN ACTIVE ADDICTION ISSUE.

Another example is that you cannot expect to be constantly negative, miserable, complaining, aggressive, silly, unfocused, making unnecessary comments, or declaring how overwhelmed you are or how bad your situation is, and expect your spouse to like having you around.

The reason this is so is that, as you regularly expose your spouse to this unfiltered, unrestrained stream of consciousness, you are losing Emotional Credibility points. Another way to put this is that they will eventually begin to associate *you* with the unpleasantness and general negativity of your words and tone; you will be like a grey cloud over their heads when you're around. There will then develop, at some point or another, a very real emotional disconnect between you, and, eventually, a physical disconnect as well.

> THEY WILL EVENTUALLY BEGIN TO ASSOCIATE *YOU* WITH THE UNPLEASANTNESS AND GENERAL NEGATIVITY OF YOUR WORDS AND TONE; YOU WILL BE LIKE A GREY CLOUD OVER THEIR HEADS WHEN YOU'RE AROUND.

A few more things to keep in mind:

Your spouse is not your mother. You cannot just "spew" at them and expect it not to affect them.

And in connection with this, people like to be around people who strike them as true, Emotionally Competent adults. That means that people generally like to and enjoy being around people who seem to be *genuinely good at handling life*, no matter how good or bad it is at any given time.

PEOPLE GENERALLY LIKE TO AND ENJOY BEING AROUND PEOPLE WHO SEEM TO BE *GENUINELY GOOD AT HAN- DLING LIFE*, NO MATTER HOW GOOD OR BAD IT IS AT ANY GIVEN TIME.

Or how about this: do you come across one way at work (i.e. competent, on the ball, present, focused, well-liked, thoughtful, etc.), but completely different at home? Your spouse is noticing and resentment is building because as far as they're concerned, you're saving the best for elsewhere and for others, not for them.

Do you do things for your spouse and then wait for them to make a big deal about your efforts? Or do you just do things because they need to be done or because you know it would be helpful, without worrying too much about an immediate, outward acknowledgement? The latter builds Emotional Credibility points, the former loses them.

Do you truly listen to and take interest in what your spouse is saying to you? If they sound negative, how hard is it for you to simply *validate* them for a moment or two? Or do you need to defend yourself right away or argue against what you think their point is?

> DO YOU *TRULY LISTEN* TO
> AND TAKE INTEREST IN
> WHAT YOUR SPOUSE IS
> SAYING TO YOU?

How hard is it for you to Listen, Validate, Ask, Comment (LVAC™), *in that order*, rather than react and comment right away because of your need to fix, solve, or end the tension you think they are feeling or that you yourself are feeling?

You should know that comments breed resentment, whereas listening, validating, and asking open-ended exploratory questions earn you Emotional Credibility points. (You can learn more about LVAC in my book *LVAC Nation!* from CreateSpace Press.)

You see, the biggest problem in most marriages is that one or both individuals are what I call *emotionally incompetent.*

This may sound offensive, but it really isn't meant to be. In a nutshell, it simply means that we, *as individuals,* often have a difficult enough time handling the stresses of everyday life, with all of our anxiety, anger, addictive or impulsive behaviors, desires, temptations, etc., and that we are not really fully *engaged* or satisfied in our work and our relationships.

Now how can we expect to have a joyful and rewarding marriage when we the *individuals* who make up the marriage don't know how to *do* life? If we don't make a conscious, deliberate attempt to learn how to live a good life as individuals, there is a slim chance we can offer much to another person, except, of course, our complaints, misery, and acting out behaviors if you'd like to count that.

HOW CAN WE EXPECT TO
HAVE A JOYFUL AND RE-
WARDING MARRIAGE WHEN

THE *INDIVIDUALS* WHO
MAKE UP THE MARRIAGE
DON'T KNOW HOW TO *DO*
LIFE?

So, for example, how hard is it for each of us to agree with and live by the following mantra? (Ready for this one?):

I am having a problem with my marriage (or serious relationship) and the problem is *me.*

If you *both* have a problem with this statement, your relationship has a good chance of ending or, at the very least, of becoming increasingly unhealthy.

If *neither* one of you has a problem with this, then congratulations! You have a great start.

At this point you should know what I like to call the "**Three-Plus-One**" rule which states that if *any* of the following are present for either spouse in the relationship, it will be extremely difficult, if not impossible, to sort things out without direct, focused, intense professional help:

The Three-Plus-One Rule:

1. physical violence

2. drugs or alcohol abuse

3. affairs

plus

an unwillingness to look at your own role in the marital problems

If any of these are present, your situation is dire, and is beyond the scope of just this or any book. Please put this book down and get professional help ASAP.

If, on the other hand, none of these factors are present, then you have what I call an "innocent marriage", which means that, although there are definite problems, they are generally the usual sorts of problems people have who have yet to experience the healing power of becoming *Emotionally Competent individuals* who happen to be married to each other. Congratulations if this is you, and keep reading!

want to emphasize to you that time spent with your spouse is not "left-over" time, it is "prime-time." You cannot reasonably expect much of a payoff in terms of joy and richness in your marriage if all that you put into it, day after day, are your "left-overs":

> Left-over energy (i.e. not much.)
> Left-over attention and focus.
> Left-over creativity.
> Left-over spontaneity or ability to plan fun or interesting things.
> Left-over positive energy (again, not much.)

TIME SPENT WITH YOUR
SPOUSE IS NOT "LEFT-OVER"
TIME, IT IS "PRIME-TIME."

In your relationship, as in many areas of life, you will reap what you invest. If all you invest are your left-overs, do not expect a great return on your investment.

▌ want you to challenge yourself to act like a true, Emotionally Competent adult by trying one or all of the following today:

–take command and offer a plan for a trip or a nice activity with your spouse

–make dinner for your spouse (this includes the shopping, but they're allowed to help clean up)

–really focus on the kids with an activity

–accomplish something significant around the house

–have an answer if asked, "Where do you want to go for dinner?"

I also want to challenge you to think about the following questions:

What are ways in which I can grow as an individual? (Here's a big hint: it will either be in your work life and hobbies, *or* in your relationships or *both*.)

Next, in what ways can I be more in command of myself? (Hint: practice what I call *adult Emotional Competence skills* such as *restraint, LVAC, anger and anxiety modulation, saying "thank you"* and *"I'm sorry", learning to stop and be present, and living more deliberately and with engagement.)*

Next question: what are some key ways I can be a better spouse?

Answer:

BE LESS DEFENSIVE AND IN-SECURE.

STRIVE TO BE MORE IN COMMAND OF YOURSELF AND YOUR LIFE *AS AN INDIVIDUAL.*

REACT LESS.

RESTRAIN MORE.

LISTEN MORE.

COMMENT LESS.

DON'T UNDERMINE YOUR SPOUSE'S EFFORTS WITH YOUR CHILDREN (IF YOU HAVE ANY.)

Also, and in connection with the last item on the above list, if you yell at your spouse or ridicule them in front of your kids, you will also be undermining the children's sense of peace and security since you've essentially taken away from them their other parent by shooting verbal holes through them.

You've left them with no choice but to either feel insecure and anxious or insecure and aggressive. Either way, you'll have a hard time with them later on because of it; and either way, they'll suffer more later as well.

When you look at your spouse, how hard is it for you to see them as someone's child; as someone who was hurt emotionally as a child? Or, as I like to say, as somebody else's messed up kid just like ourselves?

HOW HARD IS IT FOR YOU
TO SEE YOUR SPOUSE AS
JUST SOMEBODY ELSE'S
MESSED UP KID?

Even "good families" inadvertently hurt their children in some way or another and we all carry the scars, including our spouses.

Can you remember this next time you're angry with your spouse or the next time they let you down?

Can you also remember it the next time they act inappropriately towards you and you need to tell them that you love them but that their behavior is unacceptable?

Here's another question for you: if you are angry, angry about anything at all, how quickly do you jump to blaming or being angry with your spouse?

Can't find the tire jack or other tool? (*Where'd she move it!!?*)

Bump your toe on his side of the bed while walking by it? (*His fault!!*)

Forgot about an event you both need to go to tonight when you'd rather stay home? (*Why the heck didn't she remind me??!!*)

Your spouse is not an emotional punching bag. Resist this reaction.

YOUR SPOUSE IS NOT AN EMOTIONAL PUNCHING BAG.

On the other hand don't take on your spouse's internal emotional environment as your own. If they appear to be upset, you can ask them about it, but you must also learn to allow them to be upset without assuming that you are to blame or taking it personally and becoming defensive.

Sometimes people just need to be allowed to express themselves and need to be heard. So try to keep your comments or counter-arguments to yourself at these times if you want to build Emotional Credibility.

Finally, if you don't believe or like any of what you've read in this book so far, please take a moment to ask yourself this question:

Has my current reality worked for me thus far?

If the answer is "no", then I invite you to continue on to the next chapter where we'll consider the past vs. the present in a marriage. Great work so far!

CHAPTER 3

PAST VS. PRESENT

What do you do when you argue with someone? Do you stay in the present with them, sticking with the here-and-now, pointing out what it is that is up-setting you? Or do you dredge up the past, no matter how far back, and hurl it at them full force?

Let me ask it another way: when you think of your spouse, do you think of him or her as they are today, or as they were in the past? What is your *reference point* for them, i.e. how do you tend to think of them at first glance?

> WHAT IS YOUR *REFERENCE POINT* FOR YOUR SPOUSE, I.E. HOW DO YOU TEND TO THINK OF THEM AT FIRST GLANCE?

I have to admit that this last question is a bit of a tricky one, since, in reality, we humans do tend to see other people as a composite of who they are or what they are doing now as well as what they've done or how they've made us feel in the past. To add to this mix, we also reference *who they remind us of from our past either consciously or subconsciously*, be it a parent, a sibling, a crazy cousin, or whomever. In fact, this latter thing that we do is done rather instantly, often before we even know we've done it.

So you might imagine, then, how difficult it truly is to train ourselves to become more aware of how we are seeing our spouses at any given moment and to become more conscious of our tendency to see them through the prism of the past, including how they've behaved towards us and how they've made us feel. After all, we're only human.

The most successful marriages that I know of are the ones in which the spouses worked hard not to throw the past at each other during conflicts.

In my office it is quite frustrating to witness a couple who is in the midst of some sort of disagreement or full out argument, just as they are about to get somewhere useful, dredge up the past and throw it into each others' faces. People have often learned to do this as a response to feeling very uncomfortable at some point in a disagreement, and it never fails to side track or derail the conversation from getting anywhere closer to a healthy resolution.

> THROWING THE PAST IN EACH OTHERS' FACES DE-RAILS THE CONVERSATION AND ANY HOPE OF STAYING ON COURSE TO A HEALTHY RESOLUTION.

Imagine if you and your spouse were having a disagreement or full out argument about the children (hopefully not in front of them), and suddenly one spouse says, "Well, how about that time in Disney World when you did such and such?", or, "What about all the money you lost ten years ago in that stupid business venture?"

That second quote is an example of a specific destructive feature of bringing up the past: it is often not something which can be reversed or fixed and therefore more often than not gives the feeling of being *cornered* by the other person triggering an angry or defensive response. Other possibilities include a counter-attack or complete emotional withdrawal or coldness.

When couples constantly live in the past and regularly bring it up during current disagreements, they are short-circuiting a very important process, the healthy process of working through a conflict *with each other* towards an eventual resolution:

WE ARE SUPPOSED TO BE
ABLE TO *WORK THROUGH* A
DIFFICULT SUBJECT *WITH*
OUR SPOUSES, TOWARDS
SOME SORT OF PRODUC-
TIVE, WORKABLE SOLUTION.
WHEN WE CONSTANTLY
BRING UP THE PAST, WE
NEVER GET TO THE OTHER
SIDE OF THE CONFLICT
PROCESS— HEALTHY RESO-
LUTION.

When it comes to disagreements, I'll often describe marriage as a factory with lots of cog-wheels and levers. The mark of a strong, mature marriage is how it handles the debris (arguments) when they get thrown into the cogs.

> A WEAK MARRIAGE IS LIKE A FACTORY WHICH IS EASILY OVERWHELMED AND THAT COMES TO A GRINDING HALT WITH EVERY DISA-GREEMENT.

This halt can be described as either explosiveness, complete withdrawal, or some other sort of acting out behavior as the spouses try desperately to deal with the disconnect between them.

The problem is that as the years go by (if they last that long), they are constantly losing Emotional Credibility (remember trust + likability?) with each other and building resentment and disconnect. It does not take that long for all that resentment to ferment into contempt, which, I'm sure you know from your life experience, is very hard to come back from.

So what are we supposed to do instead of constantly bringing up or living in the past? The answer comes in two parts:

First, you must be able to forgive.

Second, you must deal with what is happening in the here-and-now between you and learn to come to a workable resolution to *today's* conflict.

Let's start with the first part, forgiveness. Trust me when I say to you that, through thousands of hours of therapy work with people, I've learned that you will save much time and therapy money if, before you do anything else, you ask yourself this one simple question regarding your spouse: can I forgive this person?

I'm not just talking about superficial forgiveness here, by the way. I'm not talking about: "Okay, he lost ten thousand dollars but we can survive financially from his screw up."

I'm talking about: "Alright, he's got this issue (or issues), but he's fundamentally a good person and we now have this opportunity to learn more about who we really are and why we do what we do both as individuals *and* as a couple."

Now, as you recall from what I've said before, this does not apply to couples who've been drinking and drugging, cheating on one another, or violent with one another (Three Plus One Rule), or to couples where one or both spouses are not interested in working on improving themselves.

You can't just forgive away the latter offenses; they require drastic, immediate, professional intervention and, in my experience, still often lead to dissolution of the marriage. The work in these cases involves a fundamental reconstruction and repair of *each individual* and the immense healing required in order for each of them to move forward. After this, they may or may not choose to be with one another, depending on the extent of the damage (often massive) to the trust.

So other than the exception of the Three Plus One Rule, if you find that the answer to the question, "Can I forgive this person" is "No", then you now have to decide whether or not this answer can change.

IF YOU FIND THAT THE AN-
SWER TO THE QUESTION,
"CAN I FORGIVE THIS PER-
SON" IS "NO", THEN YOU
NOW HAVE TO DECIDE
WHETHER OR NOT THIS AN-
SWER CAN CHANGE.

If, through your own soul searching and maybe some therapy or good counsel from a trusted source, together with a tincture of time, the answer remains the same, then you know where things stand and you'll now have to deal with what you want to do about it.

If, on the other hand, you find even a shred of hope within yourself that you *can* forgive, then you can move on to the hard work of changing things.

And the first thing to change is *how the two of you argue*, which brings us to the second part of the answer to our question:

You must learn to deal with what is happening in the here-and-now between the two of you and you must also learn to come to a workable resolution to *today's* conflict.

A very powerful way to begin to do this is with my adult skill of Listening, from my mnemonic LVAC™, which reminds us to Listen to the other person, Validate what they are saying, and Ask open-ended questions about what they are trying to express or what they might be feeling. *Lastly*, if necessary or helpful, we Comment. (For more details on this I again refer you to my book, *LVAC Nation!* from CreateSpace Press.)

The essence of what you need to know is that couples tend to not really Listen to one another or even let each other finish what they are saying before they start Commenting. They never really get to understand what the other person is really saying, feeling, or thinking, before becoming defensive or counter-attacking with a Comment.

COUPLES TEND TO NOT RE-
ALLY LISTEN TO ONE
ANOTHER OR EVEN LET
EACH OTHER FINISH WHAT

THEY ARE SAYING BEFORE
THEY START COMMENTING.

If you've ever tried to teach somebody something, you've learned that before they will hear you and your agenda, they must feel tranquil and at peace enough to do so. And as you also know, the way to help them get to that state is to first address and acknowledge where they themselves are emotionally; in other words, to first address *them.*

BEFORE WE CAN TRULY
HEAR EACH OTHER, WE
NEED TO FEEL SOME DE-
GREE OF PEACE IN THE
KNOWLEDGE THAT WE ARE
FEELING ACKNOWLEDGED,
UNDERSTOOD, AND APPRE-
CIATED BY THE OTHER PER-
SON.

It is like a hierarchy of needs issue: if your spouse is not feeling like they are being heard and that their position is appreciated, they will be more defensive and on alert, and it will be less likely that they'll be in a position to really hear what you are trying to say to them. What we want to do is to try to first Listen to (LVAC) and truly appreciate *the other person's truth*, before continuing on to our Comment, which is really our agenda, not theirs. (And no, sorry, it's still not keeping to their agenda if we're "only" Commenting to try to fix or solve the problem-bottom line is that when we're Commenting, we're not Listening! Comments= our agenda, Listening= theirs, period.)

By concentrating on what your spouse is saying, thinking, or feeling *right now*, you are also staying in the present instead of using the past as a defense, a weapon, or an escape. This is not only a healthier habit to form, it is also a more powerful, true adult position as it allows you to really concentrate on what this person is trying to communicate either with their words, their tone, or their behaviors. You will then be in a much better position to respond appropriately and *accurately* to them and you will both grow.

WHEN YOU TRULY LISTEN
TO WHERE YOUR SPOUSE IS
COMING FROM, YOU NOT

ONLY HELP THEM HEAL,

YOU ALSO EMPOWER AND

ENCOURAGE BOTH OF YOU

TO BECOME MORE MATURE,

EMOTIONALLY COMPETENT

ADULTS.

In addition, you will find that your "marriage factory" will become much more efficient and effective at dealing with the various challenges that life throws at us, and it will get stuck and stall out much less frequently. Your marriage will become a more robust, healing relationship, with lots of Emotional Credibility to go around as the trust and the value of the relationship skyrockets. It will grow a nice layer of what I call "emotional fat on the bone" which is a term I like to use for people and relationships which are becoming more resilient, healthier, and sustainable over the long haul.

Before we move on the next chapter, let me give you a brief illustration of two ways, one healthy, one unhealthy, in which a couple handles an argument with one another. Let's call it:

"The Big Threat, Not Really"

First, the *unhealthy*:

Sally: "I can't believe my boss is still all over me about such stupid crap."

Bill: (Commenting right away): "Well, what do you want to do, quit? You know you can't leave your job right now. We can't afford it, so you'll just have to suck it up."

Sally (option 1: Retaliation/Defensiveness): "Well, screw you! It's always been about money with you. And what about when you just "had" to take that "opportunity" back in 2003 because you couldn't deal with the stress you were in? You're always screwing us up financially, then it's my fault!"

–or–

Sally (option 2: Withdrawal/Disconnect): "Yeah, you're right, I'll be okay."

You can see that when Bill hears Sally, he's hearing a "big threat" of her wanting to leave her job. But let's see, is this what Sally is really saying? We'll never know now, because of Bill's premature Comments. Instead of Listening, Validating, and Asking, in an effort to really learn about and understand what was going on with Sally and what she was feeling or wanting to do, Bill allowed the perceived threat to rule his behavior and the results are obvious.

Also notice how Sally, now feeling unheard, misunderstood, and attacked, can either attack back (option 1), or pull away (option 2).

If she pulls away you can bet she may look compliant and "fine" on the outside, but that she is also building up resentment and distrust of Bill on the inside, along with the accompanying loss of Emotional Credibility in him. If, however, she attacks back, though the disconnect is perhaps more obvious, there is still destruction to the trust and a buildup of resentment and eventual contempt between them.

Now the more healthy approach:

Sally: "I can't believe my boss is still all over me about such stupid crap."

Bill: (having Listened, now Asks): "What's happening?"

Sally: (Now has the opportunity to explain her situation at work to Bill and she does so.)

Bill: (Validating): "Oh, I know. He can be such a jerk."

Sally: "Yeah. That's why I'm going to keep my options open. It's always easier to look for a job when you've got a job."

Notice the difference. In this scenario, instead of immediately Commenting because of his anxiety about the perceived threat of Sally wanting to quit her job, Bill simply asks Sally an open-ended question which a) tells her he's trying to really understand where she's at, and b) gives her an invitation to further express herself and figure out what she is feeling and wanting to say and do.

People really appreciate when you use this approach with them. It not only builds trust and likability (i.e. Emotional Credibility) between you, but it also helps you each grow as *individuals.* By learning to manage your immediate anxiety and need to Comment you learn restraint (another adult skill), and the other person, by being allowed to fully express and explore what they are really feeling and thinking, feels connected, validated, understood, and cared for both by themselves and by you. Pure gold.

THE LVAC APPROACH IS
PURE GOLD BOTH FOR IN-
DIVUAL HEALING AS WELL
AS FOR HEALING THE RELA-
TIONSHIP.

In our example, "The Big Threat" turned out to be more of a "Not Really" than an imminent, real threat, but you can see how the parties involved got way off track when they *reacted* based upon their initial responses to the "threat" and to each other's behavior. This destructive domino effect often begins when we Comment first, instead of Listening, Validating, and Asking open-ended questions:

In fact, let's officially redefine the word Comment here to not only mean a *verbal* comment which transmits our anxiety agenda to the other person (based on what we *think* we know about what they are saying or feeling), but to also include a *general stance or position* from which we approach the other person. We can call it "the Comment stance" or "the anxiety-defensive stance", which are both the opposite of the "learn and explore stance" of LVAC.

The Comment stance or position is one of not being at peace within yourself enough to allow you to truly focus and Listen. It is a position of needing to control or take over. It is a *reactive* stance rather than an *exploratory* one.

> THE COMMENT STANCE IS A
> POSITION OF NEEDING TO
> CONTROL OR TAKE OVER.
> IT IS A *REACTIVE* STANCE
> RATHER THAN AN *EXPLO-
> RATORY* ONE.

As we now know, the Comment stance is the opposite of a stance or position of *inquiry and exploration*. It is, instead, one of having a reaction to what is happening or to what is being said and of having the immediate, uncontrollable need to act upon that reaction. For a healthier approach in your marriage, think *explore*, not *react*.

> FOR A HEALTHIER AP-
> PROACH IN YOUR MAR-
> RIAGE, THINK *EXPLORE*,
> NOT *REACT*.

A final note, just for completeness, something which must be said before we move on. Please remember that, in the end, nobody can Validate you perfectly or soothe your internal strife completely but *you.* Your spouse can do his or her part to help you along the way (by not Commenting right away, for example), but they are not you, and they are also not your mother.

> IN THE END, NOBODY CAN
> VALIDATE YOU PERFECTLY
> OR SOOTHE YOUR INTER-
> NAL STRIFE COMPLETELY
> BUT *YOU.*

Children can hope for perfect or near-perfect Validation and soothing from their parents for a limited time as they grow up, but adults cannot expect this same level of nurturing from their spouses, who are their *peers,* not their parents.

We should instead aim for healthier, more mature communication with each other based upon truly Listening to one another and trying to learn as much as possible about where each of us is coming from, and by staying in the present as much as possible as we do so.

This way, as time goes by, we will have built a safe, trusting, resilient relationship which pays off just like any other well made investment. You may not be able to go back to that perfect understanding a child might get from a calm, non-impulsive, emotionally competent parent, but you *can* have an adult relationship which is supportive, healthy, and mature.

Now if you've read and honestly grappled with this book up to this point, I want to tell you that you've done an excellent job so far! Congratulations! Now, on to the next chapter where we'll have a look at "man-boys" and their "angry wives".

CHAPTER 4

MAN-BOYS AND ANGRY WIVES

There is a fundamental problem which most couples eventually face once they decide to commit to one another. As mentioned in the first chapter of this book, the couple goes from idealizing each other, ("oh, he is just the greatest person in the world...my true and only soulmate..."), to devaluing each other, ("that louse can't do anything right...he never thinks of anyone but himself...").

As you'll probably recognize if you haven't already, it is a fundamental theme of this book that as couples get closer to one another and become more like "family", they lose the little formalities and bits of politeness which are afforded to people who are less close to them, such as acquaintances or casual friends. The problem is that as they lose that politeness and become more relaxed with each other, their old habits and true personalities come out. And once couples stop paying deliberate attention to their behavior towards one another, the problems begin.

ONCE COUPLES STOP PAY-
ING DELIBERATE ATTENTION
TO THEIR BEHAVIOR TO-
WARDS ONE ANOTHER, THE
PROBLEMS BEGIN.

It is all but inevitable that a couple *will* go from an idealization phase, where they could do no wrong in each others' eyes, to an eventual devaluation phase where they can do no right. The trick is to try to stay on top of this evolution so that, as you disappoint each other and let each other down in both big and small ways, these disappointments can be discussed and processed *as they occur,* and the "decks" can be kept clean of too much buildup of resentment and loss of Emotional Credibility (trust + likability).

In the "man-boys and angry wives" dynamic the idealization phase has all but completely devolved into a severe form of devaluation which is often very difficult to change.

Let me explain. But first, let me assure you that, as both a practicing psychiatrist who sees his share of married men in his practice, as well as a recovering man-boy myself (most husbands begin as man-boys to some degree or another), I wouldn't say anything here that wouldn't have applied either to myself at one time or to someone I care greatly about. Nothing is meant to be insulting or degrading, but only *eye-opening* and, ultimately, empowering for both husbands and wives.

In a marriage, man-boys are created once a single man marries and gradually and repeatedly fails to adjust to married life. In other words, he disappoints his wife in *big*, sweeping ways as he emotionally shocks her with continued behaviors from his single life and even as far back as from his childhood.

Maybe he is still going out multiple times per week for happy hour or whatever hour, or perhaps he is spending just as much time with his friends and their activities together as he was before he got married.

Or maybe he fails to pick up his share of the work around the house or with the kids, pets, cars, you name it. Or perhaps it's a financial or work issue, with his inability or lack of interest in holding down a regular job or maintaining some sort of ambition or goals for himself in the world. Or maybe he allows friends to "crash" at the house for extended periods of time.

It doesn't take a genius to see where all this can lead, which is that:

Angry wives are in large part created as a result of these major disappointments or "shocks", combined with whatever they themselves (the wives) bring into their marriages from past hurts and disappointments perhaps not immediately related to their husbands but triggered by him today.

So what happens is that all of these major disappointments in their husbands' behaviors combine with and trigger other unfinished issues and resentments from prior relationships, sometimes all the way back to childhood, which then all get added up together and attributed to the husband as well. This is a very fast way to build up resentment and lack of trust. In fact, in some cases, you've never seen such build up of sheer rage towards the husbands.

And so the cycle goes: the man never truly, deliberately works on his transition to the formal role of husband, and the woman becomes ever more resentful, angry, and eventually, even contemptuous towards him and enraged: man-boys and angry wives.

Let me give you a few examples of man-boy behaviors:

The first is what I call "the sportsman". This is the man-boy whose angry wife is resentful because of all the time he spends playing in after work sports leagues, playing fantasy football, or playing cards, gambling, or otherwise focusing on regularly planned activities which do not involve her at all.

These activities, by the way, do not have to literally be sports oriented, but can be just about anything. The important point here is that they are being done as if the man-boy weren't married at all, as opposed to being done in balance with, and with the blessing of his wife and married life.

He doesn't really see the problem with any of this, often stating that he doesn't really spend "that much time" in these activities.

The problem with this argument is that, once a man is married, the meaning of time changes.

ONCE A MAN IS MARRIED,
THE MEANING OF TIME
CHANGES.

To an overwhelmed, harried, busy wife, especially if there are kids involved or a career, even a few hours once or twice a week in which her husband is engaging in some sort of activity independent of her and the project of their lives together can present a conflict. He is spending this extra time away from not only her, but from the life they are trying to build together, which should be his first priority.

At the risk of losing you with an analogy, this would be tantamount to agreeing to enroll in college or professional or vocational school to get an education, but then never adjusting to the realization that your time has now been reprioritized and redistributed because of that agreement.

This is why, when students take a break from their studies it's called a "study break". There is always the understanding that the default program is the activity of studying because of the deliberate, larger goal they've created of attaining their degree. Sure, they can take breaks, but that is just what they are: breaks, as opposed to primary priorities instead of their studies.

In a marriage, many men initially have a difficult time making the transition to fully accepting the fact that, as of the day of their weddings, they have agreed to a larger agenda and goal now: to continuously work on building and customizing a life with their wives.

Every moment now has a competing pull to it, namely, building up the married life. And if you don't believe me, just ask your wife about it. Even if she tells you, "Oh, no, I don't mind if you go bowling with the guys on Saturday nights for the next four months", trust me, there is a fairly high risk that it is going to build up into some form of resentment unless the two of you are truly in agreement about this use of your time. For, as you recall, time is not the same once you are married.

What seemed like "just a few hours a week" before, is now potentially much more valuable and high yield time spent either with your spouse, or engaged in some activity having to do with your roles as a husband and, if you have kids, a father. The man-boy never makes this jump in paradigm (though he may eventually jump the relationship or get kicked out of it); the happily married man does.

Remember: if you're over there, you can't be over here with your wife, your kids, your house, and other parts of your married life. *This* is your life now. You must get to know it and get to know her.

Another way of saying this is that a marriage cannot be approached like a part-time job. You have to stop worrying about trying to squeeze in all of your previous, single-life activities around your married life, and start seeing the possibilities for building a life you could never have imagined as a single man.

Another man-boy behavior is one I call "the social animal". This one seems to engender even more anger and resentment from the wives, than the first kind. This is the guy who tries to continue to hang out with his (usually unmarried) buddies from college, professional school, or work. It could be happy hour on Wednesday nights or meeting up with them on the weekends, all while his wife is either working, taking care of the kids, or managing the household.

I've seen this build up all sorts of resentment in the wives, who, even if they appear on the surface to be alright with this behavior, are all the while becoming more and more resentful and angry and less trusting in their spouses.

Again, the adjustment which needs to be made here is that, once married, a man's social life, by definition, is now centered around the fact that he is a married man. The man-boy does not make this adjustment and gets confused by his single-life impulse to go out and have fun with his "buds" versus the guilt he continuously experiences or the constant arguments he has with his wife back home.

ONCE MARRIED, A MAN'S
SOCIAL LIFE, BY DEFINI-
TION, IS NOW CENTERED
AROUND THE FACT THAT
HE IS A MARRIED MAN.

One last man-boy behavior I'll describe is called the "no job, no ambition" example. I mentioned it briefly above as part of the "sportsman" dynamic, but I think it deserves its own consideration since it can be one of the most destructive man-boy-and-angry-wife dynamics.

Here's the short story: unless you are physically or mentally disabled, which I'm assuming you and your wife would know about, you are pretty much obligated to engage in some sort of productive work activity in your life.

Above all, the perception by your wife that you are either lazy or incompetent will breed anger, resentment, and, eventually contempt.

> THE PERCEPTION BY YOUR
> WIFE THAT YOU ARE EITHER
> LAZY OR INCOMPETENT
> WILL BREED ANGER, RE-
> SENTMENT, AND, EVEN-
> TUALLY CONTEMPT.

Nobody says you've got to go out there and conquer the world, but you do have to be *engaged* somehow in the world.

For some, this might mean being a stay-at-home dad, and that's fine if that's the agreement in the marriage. For others, it may mean self-employment or bits of part-time or seasonal jobs. This is all fine, but you must keep at it.

If you get discouraged, lose faith in yourself, feel valueless or lacking in self-esteem and confidence, you must address these things and get back in the proverbial saddle. Especially if the agreement with your wife is that you will either be the main or partial breadwinner, you must make it an absolute goal to try to fulfill your end of this agreement.

I have seen too many wives become resentful, anxious, and less secure feeling and trusting in their marriages because their husbands have all but given up trying to go out into the world and compete in the workplace as best they can.

Again, if the agreement was that the husband was supposed to stay home and run that show while the wife goes out and makes the money, that's great. But this must be articulated and agreed upon by both spouses, otherwise expectations will go unspoken and unmet and you already know where that leads.

In the end, there is a reason why so many marriages go the way of the perpetual man-boy and the angry wife, and you need to know this so that you can address the underlying behaviors and grow both as individuals and as a married couple.

Neither spouse has to be perfect. But both partners have to be focused and deliberately engaged in transitioning from single life to married life.

And as a final note: women who *are* becoming angry and resentful towards their husbands will get much more mileage (and results!) by first trying to gently support the husbands' efforts to change instead of immediately going on the attack.

One thing I've observed about men is that, once they sense that they are already seen as failures or as having failed in their spouses' eyes, they almost all tend to become angry in return, as they conclude that they've irreversibly messed up.

I call this the kamikaze boyhood reaction: "I screwed up already so who cares now!" To help a man-boy become a happily married man, an ounce of honey is worth much more than a pound of salt. I've seen man-boys grow into fine examples of truly and happily married men and great, truly present and focused fathers with a supportive, loving approach from their wives.

If, on the other hand, this approach isn't working, or if there is just too much resentment or contempt, then professional guidance is called for ASAP.

Sometimes, as the years go by, too much builds up and people really do need an objective third party to help them get back on track.

Now it's time to look at a related topic: how to come in for a landing from single life into married life so you can create and live your best lives together!

CHAPTER 5

COMING IN FOR A LANDING FROM YOUR SINGLE LIFE

If left to their own devices, people often have a difficult time fully, if ever, realizing some of the major changes between single life and married life. I have therefore come up with the term "coming in for a landing" to describe the process of each spouse *adjusting* from their single lives to their new, married lives together.

One way to think about it is that, as a married person, you are part of a "system" now per se, so your thinking and priorities have to evolve *away* from your prior single life and *towards* your new, married life.

Let's start with some examples:

Example 1:

Single Life: "Honey, I'm going out with some friends tonight after work for happy hour. See you later."

Married Life Version: "Honey, some folks are going out this Thursday after work and I was thinking of joining them, what do you think?"

Example 2:

Single Life: "I want this new car. I'm going to go out and price them this weekend."

Married Life Version: "I'm thinking about getting a new car. It's such and such model and it costs such and such. What do you think?"

Example 3:

Single Life: "I've decided to become a vegetarian. No more meat for me."

Married Life Version: "I'm thinking of giving up meat and becoming a vegetarian. What do you think about that? Could we do it?"

Notice that the first example involves *time*, the second *money*, and the third a fairly major *change in lifestyle.*

When we are single, independent adults, we really don't have to check in with anyone about decisions like these unless we feel like it. What we choose to do with our time, money, or everyday style of living is pretty much our own business and no one else's but ours.

However, once we get married, we DO have to check in with someone else about such things, namely our spouse.

Especially when it comes to time, money, or lifestyle choices, married people have to be accountable to one another at least to some extent, in order to avoid buildup of resentment and loss of Emotional Credibility (trust + likability) with each other. Lifestyle choices can include not only diet and health issues, but also house, job, child-raising, and where to live questions as well, among other things.

You can no longer make such decisions on your own as you would have when you were single.

Whereas before, that would have been the way you operated and even survived in life, now it will most likely backfire and cost you.

Now that you are married you will need to discuss topics like time, money, and lifestyle choices with your spouse overtly, openly, and deliberately.

Then, once you agree on the plan, you must not change it without discussing it with them again.

> YOU NEED TO DISCUSS
> TOPICS LIKE TIME, MONEY,
> AND LIFESTYLE CHOICES
> WITH YOUR SPOUSE OVERT-
> LY, OPENLY, AND DELIBE-
> RATELY.

N ext, accountability and follow through. Again, different for married people. If you tell your spouse you'll do something, you must make it of utmost importance to DO IT!

The same goes for any agreed upon plan regarding the aforementioned areas of time, money, and lifestyle choices: when you discuss and come to an agreement about these areas of life, you must stick with it until such time as the two of you agree upon a change of plan.

If you do not do what you've told your spouse you'll do (e.g. keep to a schedule of mowing the lawn, taking out the trash, cleaning the dishes, washing the windows, car maintenance, etc.), you will lose Emotional Credibility points with them (again, my term for *trust + likability points*, as you'll learn more about in the next chapter.)

> IF YOU DO NOT DO WHAT
> YOU'VE TOLD YOUR SPOUSE
> YOU'LL DO, YOU WILL LOSE
> EMOTIONAL CREDIBILITY
> POINTS WITH THEM.

And as you know from previous chapters in this book, this loss of Emotional Credibility leads to disconnect in a marriage which can have all manner of consequences, including the eventual loss of both emotional and physical intimacy.

As a married person, you no longer have the freedom to willy nilly go back on your word or a decision that the two of you have made about your lives together. Whether it be division of labor issues, money issues, or whatever else, your lives are intertwined now and your decisions will affect both of you in some way or another.

Step one is to always *discuss* things in order to come to a working agreement. Step two is to follow through with the plan.

If you have a change of heart, that's okay. Just remember to discuss with your spouse your change of heart before falling back to the Single Life habit of changing things up without a discussion.

> WHETHER IT BE DIVISION OF LABOR ISSUES, MONEY IS-SUES, OR WHATEVER ELSE: STEP ONE IS TO DISCUSS IT AND STEP TWO IS TO FOL-LOW THROUGH WITH THE PLAN.

Another area of difference in Married Life versus Single Life is the important issue of *motivation and intent*.

When you are single, you are generally motivated to do things because you yourself want to receive some sort of benefit in return. In the purist sense, even when you give charitably, you probably would like an acknowledgement of some kind, even if it's just a tax break from the government. Your intention too, is often guided by some sort of plan for improvement of your situation or the circumstances of your life.

While this is all well and good we must know that, as married people, we have to come to a place where we are motivated and intend to do the right thing for each other *because* it's the right thing to do and because we truly care about the welfare and happiness of the other person and NOT for an immediate "thank you" or personal benefit.

> AS MARRIED PEOPLE, WE
> HAVE TO BE MOTIVATED TO
> DO THE RIGHT THING FOR
> EACH OTHER *BECAUSE* IT'S
> THE RIGHT THING TO DO
> AND BECAUSE WE TRULY
> CARE ABOUT THE WELFARE
> AND HAPPINESS OF THE
> OTHER PERSON.

If the only reason you are doing the dishes or preparing a great meal for your spouse has to do with money, sex, or other powerful motivators, then you are on the wrong path.

While this approach may work in the short term, such as while dating someone or for the first few years of a marriage, it will not work well for the long term buildup of Emotional Credibility and intimacy in a marriage.

The two of you will eventually come to know each other's motivations and intentions pretty well whether consciously or subconsciously. If they are truly about the welfare and happiness of the other person, it will produce the right kind of relationship; if not, it won't, and you will very likely build resentment and disconnect between you. You will either build up Emotional Credibility, or destroy it.

THE TWO OF YOU WILL
EVENTUALLY COME TO
KNOW EACH OTHER'S MO-
TIVATIONS AND INTEN-
TIONS PRETTY WELL
WHETHER CONSCIOUSLY OR
SUBCONSCIOUSLY.

As a sort of morbid aside related to this topic, I have a term I made up called the "Nursing Home Test" and it goes like this: when you're in the nursing home, will your spouse (or kids) visit you often?

I once met an elderly gentleman who visited his wife every single day in the nursing home for the last six years of her life. And I mean he *stayed* with her from open to close. They had been married for fifty two years by the time of our conversation.

The point of this "test" is that the more Emotional Credibility (trust + likability) you have built up with someone, the more true "love" they can feel for you and the more likely they will want to visit you or help you when you need them. In essence, the more you act towards them from a position of proper intent and motivation, the more they will feel cared for and valued by you, and the more they will want to be around you.

THE MORE EMOTIONAL
CREDIBILITY YOU HAVE
BUILT UP WITH SOMEONE,
THE MORE TRUE "LOVE"
THEY CAN FEEL FOR YOU.

Another way to look at it is that the more you behave like a true, emotionally competent adult in a marriage, the more Emotional Credibility points you will build, and the more you will help generate true, loving feelings in one another over time. This makes marriage an *investment* which builds in value and is worth something to both of you in the long run.

THE BUILDUP OF EMOTION-
AL CREDIBILITY MAKES
MARRIAGE AN *INVESTMENT*
WHICH BUILDS IN VALUE
AND IS WORTH SOMETHING
TO BOTH OF YOU IN THE
LONG RUN.

Be each other's cheerleader and support. When you're single, you're not really obligated to listen to and support anyone else, unless you feel like it or unless you happen to have children. When you're married, however, it becomes part of your responsibility to the other person to be there when they need you, especially when it comes to hearing them out.

> WHEN YOU'RE MARRIED, HOWEVER, IT BECOMES PART OF YOUR RESPONSI-BILITY TO THE OTHER PERSON TO BE THERE WHEN THEY NEED YOU.

Don't make the mistake of getting angry or frustrated with them because you can't fix their problem or because you've heard it a million times before; it'll only make it worse and you'll lose Emotional Credibility with them.

Instead, make it a habit to use my LVAC technique by first Listening to them, then Validating or acknowledging what they are saying or where they're coming from, then Asking questions about what they're saying. Then, and only then, should you, if you must, make a Comment by giving them your opinion or your judgment call, or telling them what you would do, etc. But first make it a point to Listen, Validate, and Ask, *before* you Comment!

MAKE IT A POINT TO LIS-
TEN, VALIDATE, AND ASK,
BEFORE YOU COMMENT!

The problem in many marriages is that we've lost our way when it comes to truly listening to our spouses. In fact it is very rare to meet a couple who even lets each other finish their sentences without immediately interrupting one another with Comments consisting of opinions, judgments, "should state- ments" (you should do this or that), and other de- structive tidbits.

Don't go down this road with your spouse! Instead, let yourself be calm inside, knowing that you don't have to have a solution or comment for them, you just have to listen to what they're saying to you. This is gold in a marriage.

LET YOURSELF BE CALM IN-
SIDE, KNOWING THAT YOU
DON'T HAVE TO HAVE A
SOLUTION OR COMMENT
FOR THEM, YOU JUST HAVE

TO LISTEN TO WHAT
THEY'RE SAYING TO YOU.

B efore we move on to the next chapter, I want to share with you a very powerful, simple goal for your marriage, which you would never really try to achieve with anyone else as a single person:

Strive to be each other's "apple of the eye".

What do I mean? Glad you asked.

You may remember what it was like when you were a child and you really felt that you were the apple in some adult's eye.

Now maybe this was one of your parents, or perhaps a teacher or maybe even a scout leader or a neighbor. The important point is that when you were around them, you knew, *really knew*, that this person liked you.

They thought you were really neat, or particularly adorable or handsome or smart. Or maybe you could tell they admired your talents or abilities. Whatever it was, the feeling was powerful and good. It made you feel special, inflated your ego, made you feel more powerful and capable in the world and motivated you to do your best.

IT MADE YOU FEEL SPECIAL,
INFLATED YOUR EGO, MADE
YOU FEEL MORE POWERFUL
AND CAPABLE IN THE
WORLD AND MOTIVATED
YOU TO DO YOUR BEST.

Now, imagine having that again. Imagine once again being the apple of someone's eye. You'd feel great about yourself, you'd be more energetic, more creative, and more free to be yourself!

In essence, you'd become the best version of yourself you could be; the self you were meant to be in the world.

Well, that's what we need to be doing for each other in a marriage. We should strive to make our spouse the apple of our eye. Hold them up as special and neat. Notice the unique or special things about them whether that be a talent for running a tight ship at home, or interacting wonderfully with the kids, or making a good living in the world, or growing beets.

> WE SHOULD STRIVE TO
> MAKE OUR SPOUSE THE AP-
> PLE OF OUR EYE.

Whatever it is, we need to make it a priority to really *like* our spouses, just like we would like someone or something very special and dear and important in our lives.

How many people do you know who seem warmer towards and more admiring of their cars than their spouses? Well, let me tell you my friend, you'll never get a better payoff in terms of true joy and peace in life than when you put your spouse in that position instead of that car or whatever (or whomever) else.

Now, I want to congratulate you for coming this far with such focus and attention. Excellent work! Let's move on to the next chapter, where we'll talk more about the concept of Emotional Credibility.

CHAPTER 6

EMOTIONAL CREDIBILITY IN MARRIAGE: THE "POINTS" SYSTEM

In the last chapter I talked quite a bit about Emotional Credibility. In this chapter I'll define this important concept more formally so that you can see how it works and so that you can begin to use it in your marriage.

The simplest way to think about Emotional Credibility (E.C. for short) is to equate it with a *deep trust* in the other person which has been earned by them via their behavior over time.

> EMOTIONAL CREDIBILITY
> (E.C. FOR SHORT) IS A *DEEP*
> *TRUST* IN THE OTHER PER-
> SON WHICH HAS BEEN
> EARNED BY THEM VIA THEIR
> BEHAVIOR OVER TIME.

With this trust, comes a natural tendency to *like* the person, since they have proven to us that they can reliably be there for us when we need them.

Now take these two elements, i.e. *trust plus likability*, and you've got Emotional Credibility!

EMOTIONAL CREDIBILITY=

TRUST + LIKABILITY

And the kind of trust we're most interested in here is what I call "micro-trust", as opposed to "macro-trust". Micro-trust involves an accumulation of trust when a person is really there for somebody; they listen to them when they speak and they have compassion and empathy for them. They don't react right away or become angry and defensive. Macro-trust, on the other hand, is pretty obvious. It involves the big, major issues of trust such as fidelity, lying, money issues like gambling, etc., drinking and drugging, etc.

Most people could easily agree when they've lost the macro-trust in someone since the issues are so flagrant; not so with the micro-trust. And yet, in most marriages, it is this latter type of trust that erodes over time, and that is why I use micro-trust in my definition of Emotional Credibility.

So, for example, if your spouse has, over time, consistently used the LVAC™ technique and *Listened* to you when you needed them to listen, was able to *Validate* your feelings about difficult subjects, and all the while used restraint to hold back their immediate *Comments* no matter how badly they wanted to tell you what to do, or tell you to stop worrying, or whatever else; when they've resisted becoming frustrated or defensive because they couldn't immediately "fix" or understand the problem- THAT would build much micro-trust and Emotional Credibility with you. (As a reminder, LVAC™ stands for Listen, Validate, Ask, Comment. And as I've mentioned before you are invited to learn more about it in my book, *LVAC Nation!* from CreateSpace Press.)

In short, when your spouse is consistently able to be there for you emotionally, it builds Emotional Credibility (which equals trust + likability.)

Now, the meaning of "being there emotionally" will vary from person to person, so part of the job of marriage is to learn about *how* each of you needs the other person and then to try your best to *give* that to each other.

PART OF THE JOB OF MAR-
RIAGE IS TO LEARN ABOUT
HOW EACH OF YOU NEEDS
THE OTHER PERSON AND
THEN TO TRY YOUR BEST
TO *GIVE* THAT TO EACH
OTHER.

If you know that your spouse feels nurtured and supported when you Listen to them and Validate their feelings instead of immediately Commenting or trying to fix, judge, or defend against what they are saying, then by all means hold back your Comments no matter how important you think they might be and give the highest initial priority to Listening and Validating your spouse. You must literally make it your business, in this case, to practice becoming better at the skills of *Listening* and *Validating.*

People get way too caught up and invested in the perceived importance what they are about to say to the other person rather than understanding that in many cases the most valuable thing they can do at any given moment is to first just Listen.

> THE MOST VALUABLE THING
> WE CAN DO AT ANY GIVEN
> MOMENT IS TO FIRST JUST
> LISTEN.

Maybe this will mean Listening for a few brief moments, or maybe it will mean Listening for ten minutes straight without saying a word.

Whatever the instance, you will learn a LOT more by Listening than by immediately Commenting and, in the long run, you will expend much less energy trying to find the "right answer". You will also be building many Emotional Credibility points.

You also build up E.C. points by improving your behavior in other ways, leading ultimately to what I call *true adult Emotional Competence.*

Suffice it to say that, other than by using the LVAC technique, we also show our Emotional Competence by just generally paying more attention to and becoming more aware of our behaviors and reactions as we discussed earlier.

Things like following through, keeping your word, not becoming angry or abusive, staying focused and present, taking care of business both at home as well as outside in the world (this includes your health), and giving your time and energy to each other are all excellent ways to show Emotional Competence or true adult maturity to each other.

> THINGS LIKE FOLLOWING THROUGH, KEEPING YOUR WORD, NOT BECOMING ANGRY OR ABUSIVE, STAYING FOCUSED AND PRESENT, AND TAKING CARE OF BUSINESS BOTH IN THE HOME AND OUT IN THE WORLD ARE WAYS TO SHOW EMOTIONAL COMPETENCE TO EACH OTHER.

Striving for Emotional Competence in your life is a fundamentally necessary step in building up

Emotional Credibility with your spouse. Notice how I said in *your* life?

That's because a very large part of being married involves the goal of *growing as an individual* so that you can in turn be the best spouse you can be. (Remember the whole idea of marriage as an Emotional Laboratory to help each *individual* heal from childhood wounds?)

You will need to be honest with yourself about areas of your personality which need to change in order to become more Emotionally Competent as an individual. In addition to seeing an individual therapist, keeping a diary and seeking advice and a listening ear from reliable friends and family can also help you grow.

The important point here is that you pause and take an honest look at your behaviors and acknowledge them so that you can make the appropriate changes over time.

A LARGE PART OF BEING
MARRIED INVOLVES THE
GOAL OF *GROWING AS AN
INDIVIDUAL*.

So, after all this talk about Emotional Credibility, what exactly is an E.C. point? An Emotional Credibility point is like a dollar earned in your bank account. The more Emotionally Competent your behavior in your marriage, the more E.C. points you will build and the more generous and loving your spouse will feel towards you in return.

Investors and financial advisors have no problem with this concept. The idea of building *value* in their investments is the bread and butter of what they do all the time for themselves and for their clients.

We need to begin to look at marriage as an investment: a long term emotional investment in another human being which, when allowed to grow over time, will provide a very high yield return on your efforts.

As the years go by and you build up your E.C. points with each other, you build a highly valuable, highly customized relationship which is unique to your lives together, not easily replaceable, and which provides much joy.

WE NEED TO BEGIN TO
LOOK AT MARRIAGE AS AN
INVESTMENT: A LONG TERM
EMOTIONAL INVESTMENT IN
ANOTHER HUMAN BEING
WHICH, WHEN ALLOWED TO
GROW OVER TIME, WILL
PROVIDE A VERY HIGH
YIELD RETURN ON YOUR EF-
FORTS.

When we begin to use the concept of E.C. points in our marriage, we have an instant, quantifiable way to judge our own behavior at any given time in terms of whether it adds or takes away E.C. points.

For example, if your spouse comes to you with an issue which is bothering her and you blow her off because of another commitment without arranging to discuss it later; or if you become angry with her or belittle her concerns, you have lost a good deal of E.C. points!

If your spouse expresses some desire or another about whatever and you do not at least acknowledge or Validate them but, instead, you judge them, scold them, or make them feel badly about themselves, you have again lost E.C. points with them.

Sometimes our behaviors towards each other, if we were talking about money instead of E.C. points, would be akin to opening up the vaults and letting the money fly out with the wind.

Cheating on each other and other betrayals, as well as substance abuse and violence towards one another are just a few examples of throwing the door open and letting the points fly out en masse. What follows soon thereafter is a marriage that's in emotional bankruptcy!

It is very difficult to re-build E.C. points with each other once they are lost. Remember, E.C. points ultimately represent deep trust plus liking one another and wanting to be around each other.

Over the years, couples continuously lose E.C. points until the relationship is like an empty bank account: no true value and you're even charged a fee just to keep the account open! Emotionally, there are no longer any E.C. points, and, instead, you've got nothing left but resentment and maybe even contempt towards each other.

> IT IS VERY DIFFICULT TO
> RE-BUILD E.C. POINTS WITH
> EACH OTHER ONCE THEY
> ARE LOST.

This is why your best bet for the long term is to become aware of which of your behaviors and responses produce *gains* in E.C. points and which produce *losses.* This will allow you to examine yourself more objectively and not take what you see as personally or defensively as you might have otherwise.

It will also help you to change E.C.-losing behaviors and responses to E.C.-gaining ones.

If your spouse is doing the same thing, you will both benefit in the long run and your marriage will build in both worth and value.

Before we end, I want to share with you a simple word which describes the act of caring about your spouse in the ways described in this chapter; one which I did not invent and one which many people use without having much of a clue about what it truly means or entails in the long term.

It is a word which we begin to hear and to use in our childhoods with our parents, then continue to use as dating adolescents, and, finally, as adults-- all the while without a true sense of what it *really means;* and without a clue as to what is *required* in order to say it or apply it to another human being *correctly.*

That word is *love.*

The bottom line is that to truly love someone, you must first have cared enough about them to have attained some degree of Emotional Competence.

Part of that work is that you must also have come to know which of your behaviors and responses build Emotional Credibility and which *lose* it.

Otherwise the word love, when you use it, will be as empty as your E.C. account with that person.

TO TRULY LOVE SOMEONE,

YOU MUST FIRST HAVE

CARED ENOUGH ABOUT

THEM TO HAVE ATTAINED

SOME DEGREE OF EMO-
TIONAL COMPETENCE.

Now let's move on to the next chapter where we'll take the E.C. concept and apply it to what I've found to be a very popular and important subject with couples: sex and marriage.

CHAPTER 7

SEX AND MARRIAGE

One of the more prevalent problems in marriage is the evolution of the couple's sex life, or perhaps we might more accurately term it a "devolution".

The unfortunate reality is that many couples experience a slowing down or even a complete cessation of their sex lives together as time goes by, and this can, in many cases, create problems for the marriage.

> MANY COUPLES EXPERIENCE
> A SLOWING DOWN OR EVEN
> A COMPLETE CESSATION OF
> THEIR SEX LIVES TOGETHER
> AS TIME GOES BY.

What is important to realize is that this sexual "devolution" is quite often the result not of physical problems, but of *emotional issues* within the marriage leading to an *emotional disconnect* between spouses. We have discussed the concept of emotional disconnect before and in this chapter we will need to focus on this again, as it is often the major contributor to sexual or *physical disconnect* in a marriage.

> EMOTIONAL DISCONNECT IS OFTEN THE MAJOR CONTRIBUTOR TO SEXUAL OR *PHYSICAL DISCONNECT* IN A MARRIAGE.

Generally, when sexual problems arise in a marriage, especially for men, the presentation is fairly predictable. They begin to complain, often out loud, to their spouses or they begin to act more and more needy for sex, taking on ever increasingly obnoxious or annoying behaviors like begging, nagging, or making constant, sometimes angry, innuendos or digs.

For women, these troubling behaviors tend to make them want sex even *less* as they become more and more irritated and even repulsed by the ever increasingly obsessive and immature advances.

FOR WOMEN, THESE
TROUBLING BEHAVIORS
TEND TO MAKE THEM WANT
SEX EVEN *LESS.*

Remember that no matter how much the issue of sexual incompatibility appears at first glance to be a *physical* issue, the underlying problem is more often than not primarily *emotional* in nature.

THE UNDERLYING PROBLEM
IS MORE OFTEN THAN NOT
PRIMARILY *EMOTIONAL* IN
NATURE.

We have to understand that, in order to address the problem, the real area of focus needs to be on the *emotional intimacy* rather than on the *physical intimacy.*

The sexual problems are only the tip of an emotional iceberg, which runs much deeper, and the reality is that by the time a couple is having problems with their sex lives, they have already been having problems with emotional intimacy, i.e. their *emotional connectedness.*

THE SEXUAL PROBLEMS ARE
ONLY THE TIP OF AN EMO-
TIONAL ICEBERG

In some ways it's very simple, as we discussed in the last chapter: more Emotional Credibility points (E.C. points) equals greater emotional connectedness, which can set the stage for a couple to experience more physical intimacy.

When you consistently put forth the effort of behaving in ways which build up your E.C. points with each other, sex becomes a natural extension of your overall relationship together. You already have the intimacy, so the physical intimacy is not as great a jump.

WHEN YOU CONSISTENTLY
PUT FORTH THE EFFORT OF
BEHAVING IN WAYS WHICH
BUILD UP YOUR E.C. POINTS
WITH EACH OTHER, SEX BE–

COMES A NATURAL EXTEN-
SION OF YOUR OVERALL RE-
LATIONSHIP TOGETHER.

A complicating factor in all this is that men and women are generally wired differently when it comes to sex. As for men, they generally tend to feel emotionally closer when they have had sex or are having regular sex with their partners. Women, on the other hand, generally tend to feel more physically intimate when they are feeling emotionally connected with their mates.

MEN AND WOMEN ARE GEN-
ERALLY WIRED DIFFERENTLY
WHEN IT COMES TO SEX.

This leads back to the original goal of building Emotional Credibility with each other through habits and behaviors which communicate a degree of what I call true adult Emotional Competence to the other person.

As we've discussed before, in everyday married life there is an accumulation of small emotional disconnects between spouses. These disconnects can come in many flavors and varieties and often have much to do with key aspects of our behaviors towards one another.

I am going to list for you some very important examples of these behaviors, some of which we've seen before. Then, I'll take them one by one (not necessarily in order however), and I'll explain them to you and tell you what you can do about them in order to build back the Emotional Credibility in your marriage. Here they are:

Lack of listening and empathy.

Tone.

Not thinking about the other person.

Defensiveness.

Lack of support.

Behaviors when overwhelmed.

Let's start with the first one, lack of listening and empathy. If one spouse is upset by something and tries to tell the other spouse about it, can they count on truly being listened to and heard?

I mean, literally, will their spouse stop what they are doing, even for just a moment or two, face them, or at least look at them, and listen?

Then, after listening, will they offer some kind of empathy, in other words some sort of kind word or other acknowledgement of what the upset or worried spouse is saying? And I mean *before anything else;* before making a counterpoint, before minimizing the situation to make them "feel better", before offering their own experience, and before *arguing* with them or telling them that they're being ridiculous. (As for that last one, we'd might as well just open our vault of hard earned E.C. points and let them blow out with the wind!)

DO YOU *LISTEN BEFORE ANYTHING ELSE;* BEFORE MAKING A COUNTERPOINT, BEFORE MINIMIZING THE SITUATION TO MAKE THEM "FEEL BETTER", BEFORE OF-FERING YOUR OWN EXPE-RIENCE, AND BEFORE *AR-*

GUING OR TELLING THEM
THAT THEY'RE BEING RIDI-
CULOUS?

This is why it is so useful and important to re-member and practice the LVAC™ mnemonic which I've mentioned several times so far and which stands for Listen, Validate, Ask, Comment, *in that order.* With LVAC you are assured of doing the right thing and of building E.C. points. At the very least you are at least assured of not completely messing it up.

Please don't try to out-guess or out-smart LVAC. For your own happiness and joy, just resolve to keep it simple and to keep it with you always. Make it your goal to try to consistently practice and hone this skill.

And for those of you sitting there saying, "Oh jeez, I thought this chapter was supposed to solve our sex problem!", I ask that you please take a leap of faith with me and that you reserve judgment for just a little while longer. Set aside all doubt right now and focus on what I'm saying here. If you do this in a serious way and *pour energy into it*, I promise that it *will* pay off for you and for your marriage.

Do this:

First, Listen. Okay, let me say that again: first Listen. Just listen. The trouble is that most of us Comment pretty much right away, and then, maybe, if there's spare time and energy *AND* if we are still talking at all with the other person and haven't yet charged off in anger *AND* if we're feeling secure enough and unthreatened enough in our own position on the matter *AND* feel that we've communicated our position to them in a definitive manner *AND* blah-blah-blah... only then, *maybe*, just maybe, we *might* just listen a bit, but just a bit!

The point of my little tirade is that we hardly ever start by *just listening.* It is a skill which we just don't practice and hone enough. Not rocket science, but seldom understood or practiced in the real world.

FIRST, LISTEN. OKAY, LET
ME SAY THAT AGAIN: FIRST
LISTEN. JUST LISTEN.

Now, if you've listened and I mean *really listened*, then let me tell you right now that you've just built up the *majority* of E.C. points with your spouse at that point. Well done!

This means that you have already given them the bulk of what they really needed from you, without interrupting or arguing with them, and that, as a direct result of this, their Emotional Credibility in you (trust + likability) has grown, so you both win!

> IF YOU'VE LISTENED AND I MEAN *REALLY LISTENED*, THEN LET ME TELL YOU RIGHT NOW THAT YOU'VE JUST BUILT UP THE *MAJORITY* OF E.C. POINTS WITH YOUR SPOUSE AT THAT POINT.

Next, after listening, you could (and should) offer some empathy or support about their feelings (i.e. Validate them.)

Then, we might Ask some open-ended questions about what they are trying to express or what they are feeling in order to learn more and help *them* learn more about what they are feeling and what they're trying to say.

Then, finally, and only if necessary, do we make a Comment.

What's so elegant about the LVAC technique is that it forces you to Listen first and to Validate what the other person is saying, even if by validating you are simply repeating to them what you've heard them say or just making an empathetic sound ("uh-huh", "I see"), or motion (head nod). These things are universally what we humans need to feel heard and acknowledged. We are all very similar in this regard, every one of us.

After Listening and Validating, LVAC tells us we can use open-ended questions to explore and to understand the other person even better; and at the same time our open-ended questions are helping them understand *themselves* better as well!

When people are trying to explain something to you, and, especially if it's a difficult subject for them to discuss, the more you can help them clarify what they are saying, the more they themselves will learn about what they are truly feeling as well. What

a gift! Helping each other learn more about ourselves like this builds Emotional Credibility.

Think of Listening and Validating as the emotional lubrication or "foreplay" necessary for the
process of trying to understand your spouse better
before maybe gently Asking them more about what
they are experiencing.

You are getting to understand them better, *but
you are also helping them understand themselves
better as well.* The results can be quite earth-
shaking and rewarding for both of you! (See, told
you we'd get to the sex!)

THINK OF LISTENING AND
VALIDATING AS THE EMO-
TIONAL LUBRICATION OR
"FOREPLAY" NECESSARY FOR
THE PROCESS OF TRYING
TO UNDERSTAND YOUR
SPOUSE BETTER.

This all dovetails nicely with number four on our list of habits which cause both emotional and physical disconnect, namely, *defensiveness.* Therefore, let's skip down to number four next.

In general, how quickly do you jump to defend yourself or need to prove you are right and your spouse is wrong?

If your spouse is trying to tell you something, do you focus on what they are trying to express to you, in other words, on *their truth*, whether or not you think it is correct?

In other words, are you trying to learn what they are feeling?

Because they are emotionally close to us, most of us tend to feel triggered by the strong emotions of our spouses or others we care about, often to the point of not being able to handle our reactions or restrain the need to immediately express these reactions to them.

BECAUSE THEY ARE CLOSE
TO US, MOST OF US TEND

TO FEEL TRIGGERED BY THE
STRONG EMOTIONS OF OUR
SPOUSES OR OTHERS WE
CARE ABOUT.

This behavior, i.e. defensiveness, together with not truly listening and offering empathy as we just discussed, are important causes of the residual buildup of resentment leading to emotional disconnect in a marriage.

Bottom line: do not be defensive. Instead, try to *understand and explore* where your spouse is coming from and try not to take it so personally. Think: "explore", not "defend".

THINK: "EXPLORE", NOT
"DEFEND".

Next let's look at number five on our list of disconnect-producing marital habits, which is *lack of support.* How hard is it for you to truly pay attention to what would help your spouse in day to day life *and to then actually do it?*

For instance, if a husband knows on a particular day that it would really help his wife if he did the dishes or got the kids to bed, why not just make it a priority and do it? I mean *really* make it a priority, as in, *pour energy into it* and make it happen as though his own happiness depended on it.

> *POUR ENERGY INTO IT AND MAKE IT HAPPEN* AS THOUGH YOUR HAPPINESS DEPENDED ON IT.

A caveat to this however: more than a few spouses ruin or sabotage their attempts at giving support by becoming resentful or giving up if they do not get an overt or immediate thank you.

Do not fall into this trap! If you do manage to give your spouse the kind of support they really need at the moment they really need it, don't blow it by becoming resentful or feeling that they owe you something.

Though it is never a mistake to say, "thank you" to your spouse, it *is* a mistake to become angry if you are not given an outward, immediate acknowledgement of your efforts. You will blow the E.C. points you've earned, and maybe more than that.

The whole point of providing support is to do just that: to learn to provide support!

We are not supposed to see this as some sort of heroic, out of our way effort, but, instead, as a basic marriage maintenance technique to keep resentments and emotional disconnects at bay and to promote Emotional Credibility and emotional connectedness.

Remember, one of our major goals in our marriages is to actually allow and to even help the other person to *like us*, to want to have us around. (Remember: Emotional Credibility= trust + *likability*). In addition, by learning to provide support, you yourself grow as a person as well.

ONE OF OUR MAJOR GOALS IN OUR MARRIAGES IS TO ACTUALLY ALLOW AND TO EVEN HELP THE OTHER PERSON TO *LIKE US*, TO WANT TO HAVE US AROUND.

So, make it a priority to pay attention and learn what your spouse needs from you.

Then, make it your business to support them in those ways while they learn to do the same for you.

Sometimes support simply means listening and showing you understand, even if you have no immediate solution to the problem.

Sometimes it just means not arguing or being defensive.

At other times it can mean doing specific chores or helping your spouse out in ways which may not look very important to you but which are very important to them.

By doing these things you will grow and begin to look like the Emotionally Competent person you need to be and that they need and want you to be as well.

This leads to what I've listed as number three on the list of bad habits, i.e. not thinking about the other person. Do you really think about your spouse?

When I ask this question, I am not referring to thinking about them in terms of what they can immediately do for us or what we immediately want from them; nor am I talking about the rote, memorized things we do like saying "I love you" or buying them flowers or other small gifts (though many do appreciate these things as well.)

What I *am* referring to here is an honest, true concern for them and for their well-being.

I am referring to the sense that you really and truly do care about them; that you'd give to them the thing or things which are hardest for you to give simply because you care about them dearly.

WHAT I *AM* REFERRING TO
IS AN HONEST, TRUE CON-
CERN FOR THEM AND FOR
THEIR WELL-BEING.

And when I say, "give them the thing which is hardest for you to give", I am referring to things like listening to them without interrupting or arguing, supporting them even if you do not immediately understand or agree with them, and doing things for them which you know are important or would be helpful to them.

I'm also talking about including them in your thought process even if they're not right in front of you.

> DO YOU INCLUDE YOUR
> SPOUSE IN YOUR THOUGHT
> PROCESS EVEN IF THEY'RE
> NOT RIGHT IN FRONT OF
> YOU?

Do you think of them and consider them when making a purchase or when choosing a restaurant or a vacation spot? How about when accepting someone's invitation to a party or to happy hour? Do you really, truly think about your spouse; i.e. what they'd like, not like, want, or not want? Do they really occupy that special place of importance in your thought process?

> DOES YOUR SPOUSE OCCU-
> PY THAT SPECIAL PLACE OF

IMPORTANCE IN YOUR
THOUGHT PROCESS?

I am amazed at how, in some marriages, the spouses can do this for their children (which I think is wonderful and very important by the way), but not for each other. They think of it as more of an *obligation* than an actual, deliberate choice to care about and prioritize one another.

There's no way around this or of faking this: to have a healthy marriage, including sexually, you must develop an actual, genuine attitude of caring for the well being of your spouse.

> YOU MUST DEVELOP AN
> ACTUAL, GENUINE ATTI-
> TUDE OF CARING FOR THE
> WELL-BEING OF YOUR
> SPOUSE.

We have two more items on our list, and one of them is *tone.* The tone we use with each other in our marriages is so important that perhaps I should have started the chapter with this one.

In fact, if there's one thing I would absolutely say is most vital to a healthy marriage it would be the development of a *conscious awareness of tone.*

IF THERE'S ONE THING
THAT IS MOST VITAL TO A
HEALTHY MARRIAGE IT IS
THE DEVELOPMENT OF A
*CONSCIOUS AWARENESS OF
TONE.*

Many of the couples I see in my office begin to build resentment and emotional disconnect precisely because of the lack of *tone awareness* with each other. The fact is that, besides facial expression and body language, people are very quick at picking up tone, and I mean very quick.

We humans are quite adept at identifying the *complex emotional makeup in the sound of the human voice.* Maybe it's a survival thing, but whatever the origins, we've developed a very effective way to quickly and accurately read other people's inner states by their tone.

No matter what the actual *content* of the other person's message, we will first react to the tone with which they deliver it, whether we know it or not.

> NO MATTER WHAT THE AC-
> TUAL *CONTENT* OF THE
> OTHER PERSON'S MESSAGE,
> WE WILL FIRST REACT TO
> THE TONE WITH WHICH
> THEY DELIVER IT.

When you hear your spouse's voice, what emotions can you immediately identify or do you think you consciously or subconsciously react to? Anger? Sadness? Blame? Exasperation? Frustration? Guilt? Shame?

After a while, we are trained to reference a certain set of emotions based upon our accumulated reactions to our spouse's tone over time. In other words, we become trained to either respond positively or negatively *just by the mere sound of the other person's voice, regardless of what they are actually saying to us anymore.* Eventually, even good news can trigger a negative reaction based upon this training.

WE BECOME TRAINED TO EI-
THER RESPOND POSITIVELY
OR NEGATIVELY JUST BY
THE MERE SOUND OF THE
OTHER PERSON'S VOICE,
REGARDLESS OF WHAT
THEY ARE ACTUALLY SAY-
ING TO US.

The next thing that happens, unfortunately, is that whenever we even *think* about our spouses, the thought of them itself becomes associated with negative thoughts in our minds. They are now what I call "hardwired to the bad." In other words, any thought of them brings up unpleasant emotions and we don't like being around them. This would be the opposite of them having good Emotional Credibility with us (as a reminder Emotional Credibility = trust + likability or wanting to be around the other person.)

This loss of Emotional Credibility becomes a major setback in the maintenance of the emotional connection in the marriage, and it leads to the buildup of more disconnect and resentment.

If the mere thought of your spouse repulses you emotionally to the point of not even really wanting them around you, how can we ever expect that you'd want anything to do with them physically? Ever?

Make it a point to improve your sense of what your tone is at any given time with your spouse, because that tone is communicating much more than you know and it communicates it instantly.

I call this "tone awareness."

With a careless tone, you will lose Emotional Credibility even before you get to express your full point to your spouse.

> WITHOUT "TONE AWARE-
> NESS" YOU WILL LOSE EMO-
> TIONAL CREDIBILITY WITH
> YOUR SPOUSE.

With good tone awareness, on the other hand, you will also learn to become more aware of your own inner state when you speak with your spouse.

This will help you to grow and it will also allow you to approach your spouse in a more Emotionally

Competent manner, which will serve to build up the trust and all those good E.C. points.

Finally, let's look at the last item on our list, namely, behaviors when overwhelmed. Each of us has a different threshold we must reach before we begin feeling overwhelmed with life, at which point there tend to be certain behaviors we resort to, which are different for each person.

Some of these behaviors are as follows: irritability, shortness, low frustration tolerance ("I've had it up to here!"), negativity, complaining, blaming, paranoia, helplessness, and hopelessness. At this point, the person is essentially on a one-way express towards accumulating resentment from their spouse, i.e., losing many E.C. points.

As I've said before, it would be like throwing open a bank vault and just letting the money fly away out the door with the wind. It is quite destructive and can be very difficult to recover from, especially when done habitually.

So how do we change this "one-way express"?

The answer is that we must do several things.

Step one is what I call "the discussion step." Once the iron is cold and things have calmed down (yes, you guessed correctly if you think it's a bad idea to bring the subject up *while* the person is already overwhelmed), the couple must find the time and the courage to discuss the offending behaviors.

Specifically, they must discuss the damaging aspects of the behaviors upon the marital trust and intimacy, and then they must agree upon a plan of action to change this pattern, which I'll describe below.

The couple must approach this discussion in an open, calm, and sincere manner given the potential seriousness of the disconnect and the damage to the Emotional Credibility that occurs with these behaviors. If you want change and greater intimacy in your marriage, take this discussion very, very seriously.

Step two is what I call "the two-step" (like the dance.)

In "the two-step", the couple must agree that when the behaviors occur again, (and this is almost inevitable for a while until healthier habits are learned), they must do the following: first, the *of-*

fending spouse must try to catch themselves in the act and attempt to *restrain themselves* from further destructive acting out. I call this "self-policing."

Second, the *offended* spouse must call out the behavior as a verbal cue that it is happening again, in real time, as it is happening. This is not meant to taunt or to punish the offender, but merely to provide help via a verbal cue to help them snap out of the offending behaviors and save some of their Emotional Credibility. I call this "reminding."

That's "the two-step" and it works.

Remember, sex in a marriage is directly related to the degree of Emotional Credibility in that marriage, so by first discussing the offending behaviors, then doing "the two-step", you help each other preserve or repair the intimacy, both emotional *and* physical.

"REMINDING" BY CALLING
OUT THE BEHAVIORS IS NOT
MEANT TO TAUNT OR TO
PUNISH THE OFFENDER...
BUT MERELY TO SAVE SOME
EMOTIONAL CREDIBILITY.

So for example, if Sally is completely burnt out for the day and is starting to pick on or criticize or micro-manage or control Johnny, then, assuming they've already done "the discussion step", now it's time for "the two-step".

This means that a) Sally must "self-police" and try to catch and *restrain herself* before more damage is done, and b) Johnny must "remind" Sally by calling out the behavior to help her snap out of it.

Remember, if "the discussion step" has been done correctly and earnestly, then both spouses are prepared for "the two-step"; i.e., Sally is ready to not feel criticized or taunted by Johnny as she tries to re-strain herself, and Johnny is not feeling afraid to call her out on her behavior by saying something like, "Honey, this is exactly that thing we talked about try-ing to change", or something to that effect.

So the next time your spouse acts out when they are feeling overwhelmed, you can ask them if they'd like to do that "two-step" you all agreed upon.

We have now discussed six common habits and behaviors which destroy Emotional Credibility in a marriage and what to do about them.

Once we address these common mechanisms of disconnect and the accompanying buildup of resentment, a wonderful thing starts to happen: the couple actually starts to like each other and want to be with each other again.

No, it isn't the same as it was when the couple was "madly in love". It's better than that. This time they have achieved a different level of intimacy and closeness; more *real*, more resilient, more fluid and self-sustaining. Their relationship has become a highly customized and valuable emotional investment which will serve each of them very well over the long term.

Any couple can experience the blind passion that comes with a new relationship. It is blind precisely because, at first, all of the ways that they will later drive each other crazy are summarily ignored at every level almost like overlooking obvious problems in a house you're about to buy because of the overall excitement of becoming a home owner.

There's a lot of romance at first, but very little actually invested at that point.

I always tell couples that, in terms of sex, marriages go through phases.

First, there is the obvious *passion phase or idealization phase.* Each spouse can do no wrong in the eyes of the other; in fact, they are each, for the most part, blind to the other's shortcomings, both real and perceived. Lots of sex here.

Then, there is the *slow down phase or devalue phase,* as the disconnects and resentments accumulate and the newness fades just as we've discussed in this chapter. In other words, real life resumes and as the disconnects grow larger, the resentments accumulate.

It is during this second phase that couples are most at risk of acting out with affairs (which we'll discuss in the next chapter), drugs and alcohol, impulsive spending, and other risky, destructive acting out behaviors. And it is during this phase that many couples divorce.

This phase also often happens to coincide with pregnancy and having children, events which tend to further decrease the desire, energy, and opportunities for sex.

You can also expect to see any resentments and disconnects in the marriage dramatically *magnified* during this time, which further diminishes the couple's chances of physical intimacy.

The classic no sex or very little sex during pregnancy or during the first couple of years of the newborn's life comes, in part, directly out of this magnification of emotional intimacy issues, or disconnects, which were already present in the marriage from the start. Now that the wife is exhausted and often overwhelmingly busy and perhaps also dealing with some degree of sleeplessness, postpartum "blues" or frank depression, anxiety, hormone shifts, and possible body change issues, all those disconnects now loom quite large and completely negate any chance of her wanting sex.

ALL THOSE EMOTIONAL DISCONNECTS NOW LOOM QUITE LARGE AND COMPLE- TELY NEGATE ANY CHANCE OF HER WANTING SEX.

As you recall, we've used the terms Emotional Credibility and "E.C. points" in this book to help describe what's been lost in the above scenario and what needs to be regained slowly over time.

Experience has taught me that the greater the Emotional Credibility the couple has with each other *heading into* these phases, the more successful they are at overcoming or avoiding intimacy problems later on. (Consider this a friendly warning and a heads-up to those of you reading this who are not yet in a marital-type relationship!)

Often, by the time a couple comes to see me, their presenting complaint is the problem with their sex lives, which they'll often term as a sort of "sexual incompatibility." One very typical scenario ends up with the wife being blamed for "lack of interest" in or "indifference" to sex.

As you now know, by this time they've already been experiencing tremendous losses in E.C. points with each other and the emotional intimacy and trust has been gone long before the physical intimacy problems began.

It's just that we humans tend to notice the problems in our marriages once they are somewhat obvious, such as lack of sex, cheating, or abuse issues, *before* we notice the more fundamental problems with Emotional Credibility (trust + likability) that have been building up all along.

> WE TEND TO NOTICE PROBLEMS IN OUR MARRIAGES ONCE THEY ARE MORE OBVIOUS, SUCH AS LACK OF SEX, CHEATING, OR ABUSE ISSUES *BEFORE* WE NOTICE THE MORE FUNDAMENTAL PROBLEMS WITH EMOTIONAL CREDIBILITY.

Having come this far, you can see that, in order for a couple to preserve or rebuild some sort of sexual identity in their marriage, they need to first address the problem of loss of Emotional Credibility.

In this chapter, we looked at six mechanisms of disconnect in marital relationships, and we learned that we must actually create new ways of behaving and being with another person when we're married.

We must accept that being a spouse is an actual, real role, just like being a parent is a role, or like your job requires you to play a role. And like those other roles, the role of spouse requires us to grow as *individuals* in order to do it well.

AS WITH THE OTHER ROLES WE PLAY IN OUR LIVES, THE ROLE OF SPOUSE REQUIRES US TO *GROW* IN ORDER TO DO IT WELL.

Otherwise, marriage simply becomes a continuation of our childhoods, which is a death knell for sexual intimacy and a tremendous loss of opportunity for personal growth.

Remember, you do not want to become "family" with your spouse, not like the family you had as a child anyway. Better to keep some sense of adult individuality, formality, and politeness between each other if you plan to keep your marriage "sexy", in the best sense of the term.

CHAPTER 8

INFIDELITY

As I've described before (see chapter 2), infidelity is one of the key offenses in a marriage, from which it is often difficult, if not impossible, to recover.

All of which brings us quickly to the point: don't do it.

Whatever else is happening in your life and in your marriage, do not cheat on your spouse. And if you've already done so, then I must be honest with you: Your situation is precarious at best and I'd suggest, for starters, that you make an appointment with a therapist as soon as you can, to begin to assess the damage and the prognosis for the future.

INFIDELITY IS ONE OF THE KEY OFFENSES IN A MARRIAGE, FROM WHICH IT IS OFTEN DIFFICULT, IF NOT IMPOSSIBLE, TO RECOVER.

As a physician, it would be natural for me to say that cheating is like a cancer in a marriage. However, that wouldn't be quite accurate.

No, cheating is more like a very severe fever or some other sign or symptom of a larger underlying disease process.

When a spouse cheats, it is often the *end result* of a broken marriage; one that either began that way or that became broken over a period of time. And the thing that is often most broken is the emotional honesty with each another and the ability to communicate it.

> CHEATING IS OFTEN THE
> *END RESULT* OF A BROKEN
> MARRIAGE.

One of the reasons why infidelity is so very toxic to a marriage is that, while it is most often the *result* of a breakdown in Emotional Credibility (trust + likability), it also serves to further *damage* the Emotional Credibility, often irreversibly.

What often happens after an affair has been discovered is that the infidelity itself becomes the focus and *the only focus* of marital concern from that point onwards. Very few couples are equipped to take the approach of getting to the root causes of the infidelity. These involve both the acting out of the offending spouse *as well as* the breakdown of the emotional intimacy of the marriage itself *which involves both spouses.*

Unfortunately the hurt is often too great for the one who was cheated on (understandably so) for them to want to look deeper at both sides of the root causes and dysfunctions of the marital relationship itself in addition to the cheating spouse's acting out problem.

THE ROOT CAUSES OF INFIDELITY INVOLVE BOTH THE ACTING OUT TENDENCY OF THE OFFENDING SPOUSE *AS WELL AS* THE BREAKDOWN OF THE EMOTIONAL INTIMACY OF THE MARRIAGE ITSELF *WHICH INVOLVES BOTH SPOUSES.*

The breakdown of emotional intimacy and Emotional Credibility is the end result of many or all of the things that you've read about up to this point *not* having been worked through by the couple.

All of that stuff about listening, validating, tone awareness, thinking about one another, coming in for a landing, growing from man–boy to real husband and angry wife to supportive wife, restraint, past vs. present, etc.–– all of it remains unknown and unconscious to the couple.

Chances are they've gone straight from the idealization phase to the devaluing phase with each other and have stayed there ever since (see chapter 1.) They've never really gotten to know one another *for real* (each being just "somebody's else's messed up kid" and not some reference point for perfect behavior or perfect mental health.)

Yet they probably treat each other and react towards one another as if they *were each supposed to be* reference points for perfect behavior, which is a setup for the great disappointments and resentments which follow, along with the accompanying decrease in Emotional Credibility and emotional intimacy.

Changing all of this, as you now know, takes conscious, deliberate work as well as the knowledge required to do the work as it has been presented in this book.

> THEY'VE NEVER REALLY
> GOTTEN TO KNOW ONE
> ANOTHER *FOR REAL*--
> EACH BEING JUST "SOME-
> BODY'S ELSE'S MESSED UP
> KID" AND NOT SOME REF-
> ERENCE POINT FOR PERFECT
> BEHAVIOR OR PERFECT
> MENTAL HEALTH.

The word "cheating" itself is actually a very fitting word for infidelity since one spouse takes it upon themselves to "fix" the marital intimacy problem by simply pursuing intimacy with someone new. In other words, they take the easy way out; i.e. they cheat.

This way they can instantly get back into the idealization phase with someone else (which includes "idealization sex" and other stimulating features), instead of achieving authentic emotional and physical intimacy with their spouse by working on themselves and learning to earn E.C. points in the marriage.

So, in other words, instead of putting in the required work into the marriage and proceeding honestly with their spouses, they "cheat".

> BY CHEATING, THEY CAN
> INSTANTLY GET BACK INTO
> THE IDEALIZATION PHASE
> WITH SOMEONE ELSE.

In addition to the common definition of cheating, which is usually taken to mean having sexual relations with someone outside of the marriage, they are also cheating by jumping into a temporary idealization phase with someone new, often over and over again with someone else, so that they can always feel those initial "in love" or "soulmate" feelings.

They never get to the point of really earning and investing Emotional Credibility with their spouses and having an opportunity to grow *as individuals*, which is what a marriage really does when done right (as you recall from chapter 1 where we talked about marriage as an emotional laboratory for each *individual's* growth).   They remain, instead, perpetually stuck with their undeveloped and raw childhood expectations; expectations of themselves (often expecting too little), and of their mates (often expecting too much).

> THEY NEVER GET TO THE POINT OF REALLY EARNING AND INVESTING IN EMOTIONAL CREDIBILITY WITH THEIR SPOUSES AND HAVING AN OPPORTUNITY TO GROW *AS INDIVIDUALS.*

Though technically a different situation, people who constantly marry and divorce five, six, seven, eight, or more times (they are not "cheating" per se) are up to something similar. They too have yet to find out that the path to joy in a marriage involves learning about and facing one's own areas of incomplete emotional development and using the marriage as an emotional laboratory to help fix those areas.

Instead, many of these people, like those who are cheating, are also chronically looking for the perfect spouse or "soulmate" who will make them happy and make them feel good about themselves.

> THE PATH TO JOY IN A
> MARRIAGE INVOLVES
> LEARNING ABOUT AND
> FACING ONE'S OWN AREAS
> OF INCOMPLETE EMOTION-
> AL DEVELOPMENT AND US-
> ING THE MARRIAGE AS AN
> EMOTIONAL LABORATORY
> TO HELP FIX THOSE AREAS.

Cheating also takes away *vital life energy*. People are only partially aware of what this means. To become fully aware we must realize that cheating exacts an *opportunity cost* from our lives, the extent of which we can never fully predict or recover from.

In other words, as I'll describe more fully in a moment: if we're using our time and energy to have an affair or affairs, we no longer have that time and energy to pour into our lives with our spouses and children (if there are any.) We have permanently lost that time and energy.

I borrow the term "opportunity cost" from economics to roughly indicate the cost to us of the things we do *not* choose in favor of the things we *do* choose.

> CHEATING TAKES AWAY *VITAL LIFE ENERGY.* IT EXACTS AN *OPPORTUNITY COST,* THE EXTENT OF WHICH YOU CAN NEVER FULLY PREDICT OR RECOVER FROM.

Each of us has only a limited amount of time on this Earth, together with a limited amount of energy to expend during this time. I call this combination of limited time and energy *vital life energy*.

If I use my time and energy to arrange to secretly meet with somebody for an extramarital affair, or to conduct an affair or affairs in general, I will no longer have that same time and energy to spend with my wife and kids.

Nor will I have that time and energy to spend on my creative projects, special events, getting together with friends and family, volunteering, or just learning to stop and be still with myself.

Even if I *think* that I am smart enough and resourceful enough and energetic enough to be able to live a double life, I can never outwit nature itself. What time and energy I expend *over there*, I cannot also spend *over here,* period. In this instance, life is a zero sum game.

Taken even further, the guilt and stress involved, over time, will eventually also take its toll on my health, both physically and emotionally.   And that's not just guilt about the infidelity. It also includes guilt I may not even be conscious of or understand fully regarding all of that missed, irrecoverable opportunity cost. It will all add up.

WHAT TIME AND ENERGY I
EXPEND *OVER THERE*, I
CANNOT ALSO SPEND *OVER
HERE,* PERIOD. IN THIS IN-

STANCE, LIFE IS A ZERO
SUM GAME.

F inally, my advice to all married people, and, for that matter, to anyone who is in a monogamous relationship is this: If you are on the brink of cheating but *haven't done it yet*, now is your opportunity to do something very difficult but very healthy and valuable in terms of building Emotional Credibility.

Instead of pursuing an affair, *guard against it* by talking about your temptation with your spouse. Though it will initially be hard for them to hear and will likely cause initial shock and perhaps anger, remember, you haven't actually *done anything yet*. And, furthermore, this issue can serve as a wakeup call and a warning sign for you both regarding the problems in the marriage and the work required *from both spouses* to address them.

INSTEAD OF PURSUING AN
AFFAIR, *GUARD AGAINST IT*
BY TALKING ABOUT YOUR

TEMPTATION WITH YOUR
SPOUSE.

In fact, after the initial reaction your spouse will come to appreciate your courage and integrity, especially if the fact of your sharing this with them also includes an invitation and a willingness to go to marital or individual counseling in addition to getting serious about learning and practicing the material and techniques in this book.

The advantage of bringing this up with your spouse is that, as mentioned above, it is an act of true adult courage and honesty and it represents your willingness to take an emotional risk with your spouse and to do things differently with them than you might otherwise have done with others in the past.

This difference is, in great part, what real adult love and intimacy is all about. Anyone can *say* (or write) the words "I love you", but do they have the true adult emotional capacity, courage, and maturity to back those words up and make them real?

Having said all this, know that, ordinarily, most people either go ahead and act out (in this case by having the affair), or they keep the whole plan or thought of having an affair secret, thinking that they can handle it all by themselves. Again, it's really a matter of not knowing what we don't know.

You may *think* that you can handle keeping thoughts of an affair all to yourself, or that you'd prefer to "spare" your spouse the pain of knowing you've been thinking about it; but, in reality, you are preventing yourself from expressing just how exasperated or out of control you are really feeling in your marriage and from addressing it with the other half of the equation, i.e. your spouse.

> IT'S REALLY A MATTER OF
> NOT KNOWING WHAT WE
> DON'T KNOW.

If, in the end, it is just too difficult right now for you to carry out this sort of conversation with your spouse, I would suggest that you at least see an individual counselor to explore your temptation to cheat as well as how you are feeling and functioning within your marriage as a whole.

Keep in mind that the wish to have an extra-marital affair is *always* a sign that, for some reason or maybe multiple reasons, you are not feeling fulfilled by and connected to your spouse. But you must also remember that, unless you are drinking or drugging, beating each other, or are unwilling to learn and to grow, there is always hope for a brighter tomorrow for each of you, and for your marriage, if you begin to take the necessary steps now!

So please, don't wait until something happens; start the conversation with your spouse today!

CHAPTER 9

HAPPY GUY: EMOTIONAL COMPETENCE

This is what many of the wives (and wives-to-be) in my practice describe to me as their ideal man: They tell me that their ideal man would be someone who *knows how to live life*; someone who has the ability to negotiate their way through their lives in a competent, masterful, and *optimistic* way, handling both the good and the bad. In short, someone who is "happy."

> ...SOMEONE WHO *KNOWS HOW TO LIVE LIFE*; SOMEONE WHO HAS THE ABILITY TO NEGOTIATE THEIR WAY THROUGH THEIR LIVES IN A COMPETENT, MASTERFUL, AND *OPTIMISTIC* WAY...IN SHORT, SOMEONE WHO IS "HAPPY".

Interestingly, on a broader scale, this description also applies to good *parents* and to good *leaders* in general. And, of course, this is also what many men, whether they know it and can verbalize it or not, are looking for in a wife as well.

Ultimately it's about trust; it's about knowing that the person with whom you are choosing to build and share a life is a competent and worthy partner.

ULTIMATELY IT'S ABOUT TRUST; IT'S ABOUT KNOWING THAT THE PERSON WITH WHOM YOU ARE CHOOSING TO BUILD AND SHARE A LIFE IS A COMPETENT AND WORTHY PARTNER.

This description of the ideal mate does *not* mean that they have to be rich or at the top of their field of vocation or avocation or whatever else. It does, however, mean that they cannot be miserable, negative, or overwhelmed all or even *most* of the time. And it means that they must have worked on, and must be willing to continue to work on, attaining a degree of what I've been calling Emotional Competence.

IT DOES, HOWEVER, MEAN
THAT THEY CANNOT BE MI-
SERABLE, NEGATIVE, OR
OVERWHELMED ALL OR
EVEN *MOST* OF THE TIME.

The idea of Emotional Competence gives us a way of thinking about how to build up Emotional Credibility with our spouses (remember E.C. points?). Emotionally competent people are *not* always acting out angrily or complaining or being negative about everything. They try to be helpful and empathetic not because they want something immediately in return, but because they just *have* (or have developed) that level of competence as human beings: They *can*, so they *do*.

Emotionally competent people are optimistic about life and are not *constantly* expressing to their spouses their fears, anxieties, or doubts about life's challenges *all of the time.*

Of course, they might talk about these things, as we all must, but not in a way that begs or forces their spouses to become their Emotionally Competent parents while they themselves come across as incompetent and out of control children.

In other words, they address these issues with their spouses the way friends and peers would talk about these things together, without the angry or blaming tone or the total and utter helplessness of childhood. They know how to ask for help or for an opinion without always having to throw their hands up in the air in total frustration while dumping responsibility, guilt, blame, fear, or anger onto the other person, which can then freak *them* out and damage the Emotional Credibility.

THEY ADDRESS THESE IS-
SUES WITH THEIR SPOUSES
THE WAY FRIENDS AND
PEERS WOULD; WITHOUT
THE ANGRY OR BLAMING
TONE OR THE TOTAL AND
UTTER HELPLESSNESS OF
CHILDHOOD.

Emotionally Competent people try their best to *work with life as well as on themselves.* This includes self-care, taking responsibility for individual happiness and satisfaction, handling disappointments, fears, worries, etc., all without attacking the other person or using a tone which communicates anger, blame, or contempt.

People who are striving to achieve a measure of Emotional Competence can use and practice Emotional Competence "skills" like those in my--

REALADULTS mnemonic:

*R*estraint

*E*ngagement in life

*A*nxiety modulation

*L*VAC

*A*nger modulation

*D*eliberate living

*U*nconditional positive regard (i.e. giving your spouse the benefit of the doubt when possible instead of immediately attacking or being defensive)

*L*iving with pain and failure (i.e. instead of acting out with substances, affairs, inappropriate spending, etc.)

*T*one & Thank you/I'm sorry (i.e. watching your tone and being able to say "thank you" and "I'm sorry" to each other when called for)

*S*topping (learning to become comfortable with just being still and present, and not having to constantly distract yourself or keep busy in order to cope with life)

In fact, these ten REALADULTS skills alone, if practiced and honed religiously, will give you all the tools you need to be a more Emotionally Competent spouse and much closer to the ideal mate which your spouse is looking for.

Let's face it: It's just human nature that people really enjoy being around other people who tend to be optimistic and who give off a sense that they are enjoying their lives, while at the same time handling and negotiating all of the many obstacles which life throws at them.

There is nothing new here. If you've read this book up to this point you've already made the connection that, in order for your spouse to actually *like* you and want to be around you, you'll have to earn their trust (Emotional Credibility.)

In the end, the way you do this is by continuously working on honing your adult emotional competency skills like the ones I just described.

In the chapter on Sex and Marriage (chapter 7), you learned that in order to set the field for possible physical intimacy, you must first work on your emotional intimacy and connectedness which is about building Emotional Credibility. With that issue as well as more generally: As you progress in your work on *yourself*, you will be building up many Emotional Credibility points.

> YOU MUST CONTINUOUSLY
> WORK ON HONING YOUR
> ADULT EMOTIONAL COMPE-
> TENCY SKILLS.

As you keep working on your skills, you will eventually get a distinct sense of actually being *liked and trusted* by people, including your spouse, which will give you great joy and satisfaction. This is the way to achieve the kind of happiness that I'm referring to in the title of this chapter.

We cannot get this kind of real, true adult happiness from another person, but only from the way we ultimately choose to comport ourselves in our lives. It is in the resulting feeling of having earned their trust and in being liked and respected by them because of it, that we find true joy and connectivity as adults.

> WE CANNOT GET THIS KIND OF REAL, TRUE ADULT HAPPINESS FROM ANOTHER PERSON, BUT ONLY FROM THE WAY WE ULTIMATELY CHOOSE TO COMPORT OURSELVES IN OUR LIVES.

We are no longer children. Children have it differently. They're supposed to get pure, unconditional love from the adults around them, no matter what they do, as we teach them and guide them along the way to becoming adults.

Children are supposed to make *lots* of mistakes, and they're even expected to cause destruction and chaos to some degree.

They're *supposed* to be overwhelmed, out of control at times, negativistic, blaming, and generally unlikeable sometimes; and even *then* we are supposed to love them. And that's because they are *learning and growing;* their behaviors are often "age appropriate."

We adults are no longer supposed to be children, especially when we are married. We're not supposed to be each others' parents. As we've talked about before, marriage is a peer-to-peer relationship where we're supposed to have *unconditional positive regard* (i.e. benefit of the doubt) for each other, not the anything-goes-unconditional love a parent has for their child.

WE ADULTS ARE NO LONGER SUPPOSED TO BE CHILDREN, ESPECIALLY WHEN WE ARE MARRIED. WE'RE NOT SUPPOSED TO BE EACH OTHERS' PARENTS.

D oes all this mean that we adults have no right to some compassion and indulgence as we work hard to grow and to pick up our learning and maturity process from wherever our parents and other caregivers left off with us many years ago?

No, not at all.

In fact, it's to be expected. But it *does* mean that we must go about this work differently than the way we would have done it in childhood.

In adulthood, and especially in our marriages, we're *not* allowed to simply act out our frustrations, fears, and inability to deal with things directly and immediately upon our spouses by using poor tone, lack of impulse control, blaming, and other childhood behaviors. Well, we can, but we'll lose many E.C. points in the process. And that's the difference between childhood and adulthood.

IN OUR MARRIAGES, WE'RE
NOT ALLOWED TO SIMPLY
ACT OUT OUR FRUSTRA–

TIONS, FEARS, AND INABILI-
TY TO DEAL WITH THINGS.

Instead, we're supposed to first practice our adult emotional competency skills, using Restraint, Tone, Anxiety, and Anger modulation, etc., *before* addressing our spouses with our concerns, problems, fears, anxieties, etc.

Your spouse is there to help you as you are there to help them, but the terms under which you can expect to get help from each other are different from the terms of childhood.

If you want to build the trust in and improve the quality of your marriage, you must never forget that your spouse is *not* your parent and that they actually have a *choice* as to what they are willing or unwilling to do with or for you at any given time. Forget this, and you can forget the infinite joys of a happy, healthy marriage.

IF YOU WANT TO BUILD THE
TRUST IN AND IMPROVE
THE QUALITY OF YOUR
MARRIAGE, YOU MUST NEV-

ER FORGET THAT YOUR
SPOUSE IS *NOT* YOUR PAR-
ENT AND THAT THEY AC-
TUALLY HAVE A *CHOICE* AS
TO WHAT THEY ARE WILL-
ING OR UNWILLING TO DO
WITH OR FOR YOU AT ANY
GIVEN TIME.

Finally, if you have children, you should know that the same principles we've just discussed also count in your behaviors towards them as well.

In other words, if, when dealing with your kids, you are constantly negative, complaining, angry, overwhelmed, helpless, or blaming, don't be surprised if your spouse starts to not like you or trust in you (this goes for the kids too.) In other words don't be surprised if you lose Emotional Credibility points.

In fact, always remember that when dealing with your children, your spouse is watching you. They are observing your level of Emotional Competence with the children. Do you solve problems or make them worse? Or, perhaps worse yet, do you make it necessary for your spouse to constantly take over the mess that you've helped create? (There may not be many faster ways to lose E.C. points than this.) Or maybe you are good about actually *doing* the task at hand, but you *complain* about it either during or afterwards? You will still have a net *loss* of points.

> MAYBE YOU ARE GOOD
> ABOUT ACTUALLY *DOING*
> THE TASK AT HAND, BUT
> YOU *COMPLAIN* ABOUT IT
> EITHER DURING OR AFTER-
> WARDS.

If you have children, part of your work on yourself absolutely includes improving your parenting skills.

My LVAC technique will go a long way in starting you off on the right foot and I invite you to read my book, *LVAC Nation!*

In addition, there are plenty of other parenting books and articles out there, as well as parenting classes and therapists who can help you with your parenting skills.

When you have children, becoming an Emotionally Competent spouse includes becoming an Emotionally Competent parent as well. If all of your interactions with your kids involve yelling, endless arguing, power struggles, defensiveness, and setting ultimatums, then you are on the wrong track.

You must work on first Listening to your kids, Validating what they're saying to you, Asking them open-ended questions, and *then--and only then--* making Comments, if necessary (i.e. the LVAC technique.)

WHEN YOU HAVE CHILDREN, BECOMING AN EMOTIONALLY COMPETENT SPOUSE INCLUDES BECOMING AN EMOTIONALLY COMPETENT PARENT AS WELL.

I won't go into the whole topic of parenting in depth here (again, I'd highly recommend my *LVAC Nation!* book for a simple, solid, and unique foundation on the subject), but I do want to emphasize that, in terms of your Emotional Credibility as a spouse, it is vital that you not come across as being in constant turmoil when dealing with your children. From the children's perspective, this leaves a memory of you as an angry, incompetent, not fully present parent; from your spouse's perspective, you will lose Emotional Credibility and they won't like you or want you around.

Before moving on to the final chapter of this book, I want to stop here for a moment and both congratulate you and thank you for taking these issues seriously enough to have read this far. It shows your willingness to *change* which is the key to growing as a person and to growing your marriage.

I also want to be the first to congratulate you for striving to become the newest member of the Emotionally Competent, Happy Guy/Gal club! You're awesome!

CHAPTER 10

FINAL CHAPTER: THE SELF

I want to close with a chapter on what I call The Self, because, in the end, and when it comes right down to it, marriage is really about The Self: *your* Self and your *spouse's* Self.

I want to talk to you about *your* Self; about how to take care of it, how to behave in a manner worthy of it, and about how to live with the greatest amount of joy and inner peace by being true to it.

We are all simply just children who have grown up in our respective families of origin, having been exposed in our early, formative years to whatever forces were at work in our childhood households and beyond. Now we are adults, and we sometimes struggle with anxiety, fear, anger, resentment, envy, rage, confusion, boredom, emptiness, feelings of suffocation, and feelings of being overwhelmed or overburdened, among others.

Some of us are well aware of these feelings and struggle openly with them and talk about them, write about them, and think about them. Others of us are *not* as aware of them and therefore act them out in destructive ways with our spouses, at our jobs, and with our children.

So much of what a marriage does to us and what we experience in marriage has to do with who we are as individuals and where we've come from as individual Selves. Unfortunately, even those of us who are aware of our struggles often lose sight of them in our marriages because of the expectations, wishes, hopes, and dreams of what a marriage is or should be; as well as who our spouses are or should be. We also lose sight of our struggles simply because of the growth in complexity of our lives when we get married and, for some of us, when we have children as well.

On the other hand, those of us who were never aware of our emotional struggles from childhood to begin with, simply continue to act them out when we get married. Then, as life becomes more challenging and complex, the acting out behaviors often escalate, as we've discussed in previous chapters.

Given the complexity of all of these factors, my closing message to you is this: Through it all, never lose track of your true Self. No matter what

Anthony Ferraioli, M.D. 203

you are going through in your marriage, your path back to some degree of peace and happiness will always lie in finding your way back to your truest Self. What do you want? What do you *not* want? What do you like? What do you *not* like? These are the questions which can bring us back to the Self.

MY CLOSING MESSAGE TO YOU IS THIS: NEVER LOSE TRACK OF YOUR TRUE SELF.

When you struggle with your spouse, find out what it is inside of you that you are responding to when the two of you talk or argue. Are you feeling threatened, directly or indirectly? Jealous? Not secure in the relationship? Or just not happy with your life in general?

WHAT DO YOU WANT? WHAT DO YOU *NOT* WANT? WHAT DO YOU LIKE? WHAT DO YOU *NOT* LIKE? THESE ARE THE QUESTIONS WHICH CAN BRING US BACK TO THE SELF.

What can you yourself do to improve things, before you wonder what has to change with your spouse? How can you address *yourself* and what you are reacting to and what it means? By talking with someone? By keeping a journal? By praying?

Do you communicate directly or indirectly with your spouse? If you find that you communicate indirectly much of the time, why do you do this? What are the strong or unknown feelings that you have that lead you to indirect communication through criticism, devaluing, blaming, or arguing? Is it fear? Anger? Resentment? Jealousy? Mistrust? Can you find a way, through talking with someone or journaling about them, to become more familiar with these emotions and therefore with your Self?

If your spouse has a serious problem like substance abuse, physical or emotional abuse, or chronic infidelity, can you find the courage to seek professional guidance and support to start to address these issues? If you are being abused, can you find the courage to seek safety for yourself and your children if you have them?

As an individual Self, what can you do *today* to take care of yourself? Of your physical Self? Of your emotional Self? How about your spiritual Self? You have an obligation, first and foremost, to own the responsibility of taking care of your Self, regardless of whatever is happening in your marriage right now.

How is your diet? Do you exercise regularly and in a manner that keeps up your interest? Do you read a variety of literature, including but not limited to current, classical, historic, fiction, and nonfiction, to keep your brain sharp and to keep yourself well informed?

Are you taking care of your spiritual Self? Do you go to church, temple, synagogue, mosque, or pray at home? If not, do you think about a universe and a meaning of life that is larger in scope than yourself and more timeless? How do you see your place in the big picture? How about your children, if you have any?

Do you nurture friendships? In his book, *The Council of Dads* (William Morrow Publishers), Bruce Feiler talks about how he chose six men from his life, good and true friends, to help his wife raise his two young daughters in case he died from his cancer. Do you have special friends like this and do they have you?

How are you with forgiveness? How about defensiveness? Do you talk about and vent about what's bothering you to someone who will give a nonjudgmental and supportive listening ear so you can feel less heavy, less angry, less anxious or afraid, and less threatened? Maybe this will help you to forgive or at least to not be as defensive.

Staying angry at someone or holding a grudge for too long is not good for your health. It also gives the other person a tremendous amount of power and control over you. Would you rather get revenge, regardless of what it costs you? Or can you let it go and move on after talking with someone about your feelings and what you might fear or perceive is at stake?

STAYING ANGRY AT SOME-
ONE OR HOLDING A
GRUDGE FOR TOO LONG IS

NOT GOOD FOR YOUR
HEALTH. IT ALSO GIVES
THE OTHER PERSON A TRE-
MENDOUS AMOUNT OF
POWER AND CONTROL
OVER YOU.

C an your Self remain present, calm, and focused? With your spouse? With your
children? How about at your job, including
running and maintaining your household?
When you are feeling lost or anxious or
bored, can you lose yourself in others? Can you perhaps take the time to connect with someone and listen to their stories or troubles? Or, if you have kids,
can you lose yourself in what they are doing or saying right now? Can you take charge and plan a special day trip or a special meal or time together?

If you have dreams or passions, do you make
the time and the deliberate plans to pursue them?
Do you try to follow your talents, and make time to
nurture and grow them on a regular basis?

When you are feeling good about yourself and your life, are you *generous* with others (including your spouse) with those feelings? Do you share your true, joyous, energized, adult competent Self with them? How about the larger community around you? Can you do something for someone for free today or with no strings attached? How about within the next week? The next month? Have you ever volunteered your time and your talents to others when you can?

> ARE YOU *GENEROUS* WITH
> OTHERS (INCLUDING YOUR
> SPOUSE)?

D o you work on the adult skill of Listening? Is it a priority for you as much as speaking or taking action is? When somebody speaks to you, are you able to forget yourself and your impressions or judgments about what they are saying and truly Listen to them? Can you try to learn about *their* truest Selves and to help them feel heard, even if you don't have a solution to their immediate problem or understand it fully?

ARE YOU ABLE TO FORGET
YOURSELF AND YOUR IM-
PRESSIONS OR JUDGMENTS
ABOUT WHAT THEY ARE
SAYING AND TRULY *LISTEN*
TO THEM?

If the person who is talking is your spouse, how does this make you behave differently? Are you more defensive? More angry? More likely to interrupt? More likely to make fun or to not take them seriously? Less likely to remember what they are saying? If so, why?

Do you truly believe, in your deepest heart of hearts, that Listening is the way to gain the trust and affection of those around you and to show them true adult love? Do you know that you will also feel more connected to them and that you will feel better about them as well?

DO YOU TRULY BELIEVE, IN
YOUR DEEPEST HEART OF
HEARTS, THAT LISTENING IS
THE WAY TO GAIN THE

TRUST AND AFFECTION OF

THOSE AROUND YOU AND

TO SHOW THEM TRUE

ADULT LOVE?

W hen you think about your life, do you think of a beginning, a middle, and an end? How do you picture those things? Assuming that you are in the "middle" of life right now, what do you want the rest of it to look like? How can you *deliberately* put things in your life that you *want* there and avoid putting things in your life that you *do not want?*

HOW CAN YOU *DELIBERA-*

TELY PUT THINGS IN YOUR

LIFE THAT YOU *WANT*

THERE AND AVOID PUTTING

THINGS IN YOUR LIFE THAT

YOU *DO NOT WANT?*

When you are at the end of your life, how will you look back on your behavior, your choices of activities, and on your relationships? Will you be proud of them and be at peace with them? Will they allow you the tranquility and comfort to die graciously and as a good example for those still living?

We tend to die as we have lived. Will you do so as a true, emotionally competent adult Self if you are physically and mentally able to at that time? Will you have lived as a competent, true adult Self so that others will *want* to help take care of you and see you off because they *love you*, and not because of guilt, obligation, or fear?

> WE TEND TO DIE AS WE
> HAVE LIVED.

Finally, I want to leave you with the absolute and unquestionable sense that you *are* loved. Though we most likely do not know each other personally, I want to send you my love. One of the most powerful, most enduring, and most healing gifts we can give to one another as true, emotionally competent adult Selves is our love.

Yes, it is love we give through our *words*, but it is more than that: It is also our love *through our emotionally competent behaviors.* And it is our love through the promise of our continuous endeavor towards Self improvement and growth so that we can *do* more, *learn* more, *feel* more, *help* more, and *connect* more in our lives.

> ONE OF THE MOST POWERFUL, MOST ENDURING GIFTS WE CAN GIVE TO ONE ANOTHER AS TRUE, EMOTIONALLY COMPETENT ADULT SELVES IS OUR LOVE; IT IS OUR LOVE THROUGH OUR WORDS, *BUT IT IS ALSO OUR LOVE THROUGH OUR BEHAVIORS.*

I want to thank you for reading this book. And I want to wish you good health, peace, joy, and tranquility.

And if you are married or are about to get married, I also want to wish you both endless happiness and prosperity in your lives together.

You can learn more about Dr. Ferraioli and his books at the following websites:

www.LVACNation.com

www.DrFerraioli.com

He also writes a blog called "LVAC Blog" which you can follow on his websites or on facebook.

Dr. Ferraioli's books are available through most on-line retailers or by special order at your local bookstore or library.

Other titles include:

Cobwebs And Ugly Wallpaper

LVAC Nation!

6913283R0

Made in the USA
Charleston, SC
23 December 2010